The Best Places To Kiss In Southern California

SECOND EDITION

"More delightful travel hints abound in *The Best Places To Kiss*. Be sure to include this one in your travel collection."

San Francisco Examiner

"No matter how distant or exotic the destination, you will find it in this beguiling book."

The Toronto Star

"This travel series will help you plan your next vacation, using your heart as a guide. There's even a listing of great outdoor locations and a miscellaneous category—for places you can kiss anytime."

First for Women

"Never has a travel book had so much heart-stirring fun cover-to-cover."

Santa Rosa Press Democrat

"If you need a place for that special occasion, you are sure to find what your hearts need inside."

Oakland Tribune

"Our hearts went pit-a-pat when we received our kissing guide."

The New Yorker

Other Books in THE BEST PLACES TO KISS... Series

The Best Places To Kiss In The Northwest $10.95

The Best Places To Kiss In Northern California $10.95

The Best Places To Kiss In And Around New York City $10.95

Any of these books can be ordered directly from the publisher. Please send a check or money order for the total amount of the books, plus $1.50 for shipping and handling per book ordered, to:

Beginning Press
5418 South Brandon
Seattle, Washington 98118

The Best Places To Kiss In Southern California

SECOND EDITION

by
Paula Begoun and Deborah Brada

Beginning Press

Art Direction and Production: Lasergraphics
Cover Design: Rob Pawlak
Typography: Lasergraphics
Editor: Miriam Bulmer
Printing: Publishers Press, USA
Contributors: Shana Engle

Copyright 1990, 1992 by Paula Begoun
First Edition: June 1990
Second Edition: June 1992
1 2 3 4 5 6 7 8 9 10

Best Places To Kiss™

is a registered trademark of Beginning Press
ISBN 1-877988-05-7

This book is distributed to the U.S. book trade by:
Publisher's Group West
4065 Hollis Street
Emeryville, California 94608
(800) 788-3123

This book is distributed to the Canadian book trade by:
Raincoast Books
112 East Third Avenue
Vancouver, British Columbia V5T 1C8
Canada

Special Acknowledgment

To Avis Begoun, for her extremely creative and romantic original idea for this book.

Dedication

Kissing is a fine art. To our partners, who helped us hone our craft.

Publisher's Note

Travel books have many different formats and criteria for the places they include. We would like the reader to know that this book is not an advertising vehicle. As is true in all the *Best Places To Kiss* books, none of the businesses included here were charged fees, nor did they pay us for their review. This book is a sincere effort to highlight those special parts of the region that are filled with romance and splendor. Sometimes the places listed—restaurants, inns, lounges, lodges, hotels, and bed and breakfasts—were created by people. Sometimes these places are untouched by people and simply created by G-d for us to enjoy. Wherever you go, be gentle with each other and gentle with the earth.

The recommendations in this collection were the final decision of the publisher, but we would love to hear what you think. It is our desire to be a reliable source for your amorous outings, and, in this quest for blissful sojourns, your romantic feedback assists greatly in increasing our accuracy and resources for information. Please feel free to write Beginning Press if you have any additional comments, criticisms, or cherished memories of your own from a place we directed you to or a place you discovered on your own.

We would love to hear from you!

Beginning Press
5418 South Brandon
Seattle, Washington 98118

> "As usual with most lovers in the city,
> they were troubled by the lack of that
> essential need of love—a meeting place."
> *Thomas Wolfe*

"You know I'd rather be lost in love than found."

Michael Tomlinson

TABLE OF CONTENTS

THE FINE ART OF KISSING 1

Why It's Still Best To Kiss In Southern California 1
You Call This Research?. 1
What Isn't Romantic 2
Rating Romance. 3
Kiss Ratings 4
Cost Ratings 4
What If You Don't Want To Kiss? 5

THE CENTRAL COAST 9

GREATER LOS ANGELES 39

ORANGE COUNTY 91

CATALINA ISLAND 127

LAKE ARROWHEAD AND BIG BEAR 131

PALM SPRINGS 143

SAN DIEGO COAST 149

SAN DIEGO INLAND 191

WORTH THE TRIP FROM SAN DIEGO 213

PERSONAL DIARY 221

INDEX 223

> "Love, the magician, knows this little trick whereby two people walk in different directions yet always remain side by side."
>
> Hugh Prather

THE FINE ART OF KISSING

Why It's Still Best To Kiss In Southern California

It must be the sunshine that affects the heart so warmly here in Southern California. There is a passionate attachment to this region that is evident in both the density of population and the vast number of tourists who visit each year. From the village of Cambria to the legendary climate and setting of Santa Barbara, from the intense love/hate relationship with the urban paradise/blight of Los Angeles to the towering San Bernardino Mountains, from the flat parched desert that leads to the urban oasis of Palm Springs to the flawless scenery that surrounds San Diego—there is enough amorous territory here to ignite romantic fires in the most cynical among us.

If you've ever longed for a magical place where you can share closeness and private moments, you will find it in Southern California: silky white beaches, crashing surf, state-of-the-art wineries, hot-air balloon rides, stunning bed and breakfasts, enticing restaurants, enthralling vistas, lush country hikes, and hidden parks—all accompanied by sparkling blue skies. Southern California is not a secret, but the extraordinarily romantic parts of this region can be difficult to uncover. Now that most of the lip work has been done for you, the only challenge left will be to find the lovable niche in which your hearts fit best.

You Call This Research?

This book was undertaken primarily as a journalistic effort. It is the product of earnest interviews, travel, and careful investigation and observation. Although it would have been nice, even preferable, kissing was not the major research method used to select the locations listed in this book. If smooching had been the determining factor, several inescapable problems would have developed. First, we would still be researching, and this book would be just a good idea, some breathless moments, random notes, and nothing more. Second, depending on the mood of the moment, many kisses might have occurred in places that do not meet the requirements of this travel guide. Therefore, for both practical and physical reasons, more objective criteria had to be established.

You may be wondering, if we did not kiss at every location during our research, how we could be certain that a particular place was good for such an activity? The answer is that we employed our reporters' instincts to evaluate the heartfelt, magnetic pull of each place visited. If, upon examining a place, we felt a longing inside for our special someone to share what we had discovered, we considered this to be as reliable as a kissing analysis. In the final evaluation, I can guarantee that once you choose where to go from among any of the places listed, you will be assured of some degree of privacy, a beautiful setting, heart-stirring ambience, and first-rate accommodations. When you get there, what you do romantically is up to you and your partner.

What Isn't Romantic

You may be skeptical about the idea that one location is more romantic than another. You may think, "Well, it isn't the setting, it's who you're with that makes a place special." And you'd be right. But aside from the chemistry that exists between the two of you without any help from us, there are some locations that can facilitate and enhance that chemistry, just as there are some that discourage and frustrate the magic in the moment.

For example, holding hands over a hamburger and fries at McDonald's might be, for some, a blissful interlude. But the french-fry fight in full swing near your heads and the preoccupied employee who took a year and a day to get your order will put a damper on heart-throb stuff for most of us, even the most adoring. No, location isn't everything; but when a certain type of place combines with all the right atmospheric details, including the right person, the odds are better for achieving unhindered and uninterrupted romance.

With that in mind, here is a list of things that were considered to be not even remotely romantic: olive green or orange carpeting (especially if it is mildewed or dirty); anything overly plastic or overly veneered; an abundance of neon (even if it is very art deco or very neo-modern); most tourist traps; restaurants with no-smoking sections that ignore their own policy; overpriced hotels with impressive names and motel-style accommodations; discos; the latest need-to-be-seen-in nightspots; restaurants with officious, sneering waiters; and, last but not least, a roomful of people discussing the stock market or the hottest and latest business acquisition in town.

Above and beyond these unromantic location details, unromantic *behavior* can negate the affection potential of even the most majestic surroundings. These are mood killers every time: any amount of moaning over the weather; creating a scene over the quality of the food or service, no matter how justified; worrying about work; getting angry about traffic; incessant backseat driving, no matter how warranted; groaning about heartburn and other related symptoms, no matter how painful or justified.

Rating Romance

The three major factors that determined whether or not we included a place were:
1. Surrounding splendor
2. Privacy
3. Tug-at-your-heartstrings ambience

Of these factors, "surrounding splendor" and "privacy" are fairly self-explanatory; "heart-tugging ambience" can probably use some clarification. Wonderful, loving environments require more than just four-poster beds covered with down quilts and lace pillows, or tables decorated with white tablecloths and nicely folded linen napkins. Instead, there must be more plush or other engaging features that encourage intimacy and allow for uninterrupted affectionate discussions. For the most part, ambience was rated according to degree of comfort and number of gracious appointments, as opposed to image and frills.

If a place had all three factors going for it, inclusion was automatic. But if one or two of those criteria were weak or nonexistent, the other feature(s) had to be superior for the location to be included. For example, if a breathtakingly beautiful panoramic vista was inundated with tourists and children on field trips, it was not included. If a fabulous bed and breakfast was set in a less-than-desirable location, it would be included if, and only if, its interior was so wonderfully inviting and cozy that the outside world no longer mattered.

Kiss Ratings

If you've flipped through this book and noticed the miniature lips that follow each entry, you're probably curious about what they mean. The rating system notwithstanding, *all* of the places listed in this book are wonderfully special places to be, all of them have heart-pleasing details, all are worthwhile, enticing places to visit. The tiny lips indicate our personal preferences and nothing more. They are a way of indicating just how delightfully romantic a place is and how pleased we were with our experience during our visit. The number of lips awarded each location indicates:

❤ *Romantic Possibilities*
❤❤ *Very Romantic*
❤❤❤ *Irresistible*
❤❤❤❤ *Sublime*

Cost Ratings

We have included additional ratings to help you determine whether your lips can afford to kiss in a particular restaurant, hotel, or bed and breakfast (almost all of the outdoor places are free; some charge a small fee). The price for overnight accommodations is always based on double occupancy; otherwise there wouldn't be anyone to kiss. Eating establishment prices are based on a full dinner for two, excluding liquor, unless otherwise indicated. Because prices and business hours change, it is always advisable to call each place you consider visiting, so your lips will not end up disappointed.

Restaurants

Inexpensive	Under $25
Moderate	$25 to $50
Expensive	$50 to $80
Very Expensive	$80 to $110
Unbelievably Expensive	$110 and up

Lodgings

Very Inexpensive	Under $75
Inexpensive	$75 to $90
Moderate	$90 to $125
Expensive	$130 to $175
Very Expensive	$185 to $240
Unbelievably Expensive	$250 and up

What If You Don't Want To Kiss?

For most couples, romance isn't easy. Some people I interviewed resisted the idea of best kissing locales. Their resistance stemmed from expectation worries: they were apprehensive that once they arrived at the place of their dreams, they'd never get the feeling they thought they were supposed to have. They imagined spending time setting up itineraries, taking extra time to get ready, making the journey to the promised land, and, once they were there, not being swept away in a flourish of romance. Their understandable fear was, What happens if nothing happens? Because in spite of the best intentions, even with this book in hand, romance is not easy.

Having experienced situations like this more than once in my life, I empathize, but I'm prepared with solutions. To prevent this anticlimactic scenario from becoming a reality and to help you survive a romantic outing, consider the following suggestions. When you make decisions about where and when to go, pay close attention to details; talk over your preferences and discuss your feelings about them. For some people there is no passion in a fast pre-theater dinner that is all but inhaled, or in walking farther than expected in overly high, high heels, or in finding a place closed because its hours have changed. Keep in mind the difficulties in second-guessing traffic patterns in Los Angeles, along the coast, and elsewhere in Southern California. My strong recommendation, although I know this is not easy, is to avoid scheduling a romantic outing too tightly or you will be more assured of a headache than an affectionate interlude.

Do not discuss money, family, or the kids. If you have a headache, take some aspirin now and not later. Regardless of how good-looking the person at the next table is, remember that distractions are never considered to be in romantic good taste. How different factors might affect your lips, not to mention your mood, is something to agree on before you head out the door, not after—or during.

Remember that part of the whole experience of an intimate time together is to allow whatever happens to be an opportunity to let affection reign. Regardless of what takes place, that is what is romantic. For example, remember the incredibly intense scene in the film *Body Heat* where Kathleen Turner is standing in the hall and William Hurt smashes through the door (even though it appears to be unlocked) and rushes into her waiting arms, tumbling them both to the floor? Well, how romantic would it have been if Kathleen had started fretting about having to clean up the broken glass, get the door fixed, and repair her torn underwear? Or remember the scene between Kevin Costner and Susan Sarandon in *Bull Durham* where he throws his full cereal bowl against the wall, cleans the kitchen table with a sweep of his arm, then picks Susan up and throws her passionately on the table? How romantic would that have been if Kevin had started complaining about the broken china in his hair and the spilled milk running down his arms? Get the idea?

So, if the car breaks down, the waiter is rude to you, your reservations get screwed up, or both of you tire out and want to call it a day, you can still be endearing and charming. Really, it only takes an attitude change to turn any dilemma into a delight.

> *"Love, like fire, can only exist in eternal movement, and love ceases to live as soon as it ceases hoping and fearing."*
>
> La Rochefoucard

> *"When you're in love everything gradually changes meaning."*
>
> Ignazio Silone

CENTRAL COAST

Cambria

Just 230 miles south of San Francisco and 230 miles north of Los Angeles, Cambria is located at a midpoint on the Central Coast, straddling Highway 1. Perhaps it is the distance from these two major urban areas that has kept everything here so pristine and underdeveloped. You won't find urban sprawl in this part of the world. At least not yet.

It's hard to imagine any stretch of shoreline in Southern California (aside from a hard-to-reach state park or forest) that you could call quaint or cozy or secluded. Cambria is perhaps the last refuge of its kind along the sylvan coastal waters of California. For now Cambria has defied developers, although I doubt that will last long. But while it lasts, Cambria is as charming a town as you are likely to find and now is the time to take advantage of it.

In spite of all these words of praise, don't be misled. High season (April to October) can be intensely crowded, though nothing in comparison to Pismo Beach or Santa Barbara, a little farther south along the coast, or Carmel and Monterey to the north. Cambria is just too small to accommodate the truly large numbers. As you would expect, the most scintillating romantic time here is off-season. November to March is the time to discover the shore, where sea lions bask on rocky outcroppings in the afternoon sun or whales pass by on their biannual migration. Or you can wander through the weathered wood-frame stores of the town and do a little window shopping. Either way, it's a great spot to learn what getting away from it all really means.

◆ **Romantic Note:** Cambria is known for its proximity to the exceedingly opulent, ostentatiously palatial **HEARST CASTLE**, San Simeon, (800) 444-7275. The daily tours through the legendary estate of newspaper publisher and magnate William Randolph Hearst take between two to three hours and cover much of the 165 rooms and 127 acres of gardens, terraces, pools, and walkways. Every inch is a magnificent testimonial to the craftspeople and architect who spent 28 years building the mountain castle Hearst called La Cuesta Encantada. It isn't the least bit romantic, but it is unquestionably fascinating. Just the sheer fantasies that are ignited after you glimpse this real-life Xanadu will last a lifetime. The $15 admission fee is worth every penny.

Hotel/Bed and Breakfast Kissing

BEACH HOUSE, Cambria   ❦❦
6360 Moonstone Beach Drive
(805) 927-3136
Moderate to Expensive

From Highway 1, turn west onto Windsor Boulevard. A short drive brings you to Moonstone Beach Drive, where you turn north to the bed and breakfast.

The nine rooms in this appealing, country-style, extremely comfortable bed and breakfast have a unique advantage over many of the other bed and breakfasts in the area: their neighbor is the Pacific Ocean. Some of the rooms have partial views, while others have a full window showcase of the shoreline, directly across the street. Two of the rooms, located in a non-view cottage at the back of the house, have their own private entrance. Each room has a small sitting area and private bath. A full, nicely presented breakfast and evening wine and hors d'oeuvres are served in the common room on the second floor, but don't be misled: there is nothing common about it. The towering wood-beamed ceiling and massive stone fireplace are framed by a wraparound panoramic window that leads out to a huge wood deck. There is plenty of room here for snuggling close and enjoying the ocean air.

◆ **Romantic Warning: MOONSTONE BEACH DRIVE** is a small stretch of road bordered on one side by the magnificent ocean and on the other by a row of tightly packed inns, motels, and bed and breakfasts. Although the accommodations here offer the best combination of location and quality, the thoroughfare gets busy when the crowds arrive during summer and most weekends throughout the year. It's not what I would call the least bit private or secluded, and you may find the kissing potential of the area diminished a notch or two. I wish I could say it weren't so, but it is.

BLUE DOLPHIN INN, Cambria
6470 Moonstone Beach Drive
(805) 927-3300
Inexpensive to Very Expensive

SAND PEBBLES INN, Cambria
6252 Moonstone Beach Drive
(805) 927-5600
Inexpensive to Very Expensive

From Highway 1, turn west onto Windsor Boulevard. A short drive brings you to Moonstone Beach Drive, where you turn north to both of these bed and breakfasts.

One of the best ways to take advantage of the graceful shoreline of Cambria is to stay at either of these picture-perfect inns located across the street from the blue waters of the Pacific. The designer of these two inns included every detail necessary for a soothing, leisurely getaway. Everything is as cozy and plush as you could hope for in an exclusive, intimate getaway. All of the rooms have enchanting ceiling canopies over the bed, pastel country fabrics and linens, cozy breakfast nooks, and all the amenities you would expect to find in an upscale hotel, such as a mini-refrigerator (discreetly hidden from view), hair dryer, and roomy tiled bath. Some of the rooms even have large whirlpool baths, fireplaces, sweeping ocean views, and garden patios. In the morning guests are served a generous continental breakfast of fresh baked pastries and fresh fruit. Whichever room you find yourself in during your stay, you won't be disappointed.

THE BLUE WHALE INN, Cambria
6736 Moonstone Beach Drive
(805) 927-4647
Moderate to Expensive

From Highway 1, turn west onto Windsor Boulevard. A short drive brings you to Moonstone Beach Drive, where you turn north to the bed and breakfast.

Each of the six rooms in this captivating bed and breakfast is a tranquil, lavish mini-suite where lovers can spend affectionate time together surrounded by fine, elegant comforts: ocean views, extravagantly canopied beds, handsome armoires, fireplaces, comfy love seats, country-style fabrics, large soaking tubs, and private entrances. The dining room and common living room have a panoramic ocean view and are throughly charming places to relax. Breakfast is a sumptuous array of such delectables as gingerbread pancakes with lemon sauce, Belgian waffles, and fresh baked pastries. Wine and hors d'ouevres in the afternoon are equally lavish. You will find that every corner here tends to matters of the heart quite nicely.

THE J. PATRICK HOUSE, Cambria
2990 Burton Drive
(805) 927-3812
Moderate

Just off Highway 1, turn east onto Burton Drive to the bed and breakfast.

Located in a tranquil neighborhood setting amid the hills of Cambria and surrounded by trees, this unusual bed and breakfast feels very secluded. The main house is an authentic log cabin. Inside, next to a wood-burning fireplace or on the glass-enclosed porch, you are served a generous continental breakfast in the morning and wine and hors d'oeuvres in the evening. A flower-lined pathway leads to the guest rooms, which are in a separate cottage behind the house. Each room has a wood-burning fireplace and is simply designed yet totally comfortable. If you wish to get away from the crowds at the beach, you won't do better than the J. Patrick House.

Restaurant Kissing

THE LITTLE HOUSE ON
BRIDGE STREET, Cambria
4286 Bridge Street
(805) 927-5753
Moderate

From Main Street, turn east onto Bridge Street to the restaurant.

Generally, I am suspicious of any place that uses words such as "rustic" to describe itself. Rustic can sometimes mean anything from broken-down second-hand furnishings to no budget to refurbish. None of that applies to The Little House on Bridge Street. This restaurant artfully enhances a historic home with new fabrics and fresh colors. The red wood-frame exterior is set off by a white picket fence and white shutters. The interior is covered with floral wallpaper, and curtains drape the stylish arched entries that open into the dining rooms. The food is some of the best in the area. Breakfast and lunch are served Tuesday through Saturday, and dinner Thursday through Sunday. Breakfast is a particularly affectionate time to discover this charming out-of-the way corner of Cambria.

ROBINS, Cambria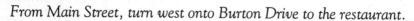
4095 Burton Drive
(805) 927-5007
Inexpensive

From Main Street, turn west onto Burton Drive to the restaurant.

From the outside, Robins looks like a congenial country home surrounded by trees, foliage, and thick wraparound vines. Inside you may feel you've walked back into the 1960s. Wood tables, a casual atmosphere, and a natural-minded, gourmet menu add to the eclectic allure. The entries, which include Indonesian-style soycake stir-fried with onions, garlic, and chiles, and whole-wheat burritos filled with cheese and black beans, are delicious. Sit outside, where you will be warmed by the well-spaced heat lamps and embraced by the meandering vines. One hesitation: the service can be a bit erratic, but if you're patient, you won't care.

THE SOW'S EAR, Cambria
2248 Main Street
(805) 927-4865
Moderate

On Main Street.

It's hard to mix elegant and casual without doing too much of one and not enough of the other. The Sow's Ear brings the two together very nicely in this charming brick-walled dining spot. Who says you can't make a silk purse out of a sow's ear? Fresh baked bread starts the meal, followed by something from the traditional, hearty menu—say, fresh salmon baked in parchment or fresh pasta. In Cambria, this is where you go to find the best in gourmet cuisine.

THE TEA COZY, Cambria
604 Main Street, Suite D
(805) 927-8765
Inexpensive

On Main Street, set back in a small group of shops.

It doesn't get much more authentic or more petite than this authentically British corner of the Central Coast. Breakfast is a refreshing assortment of granola, yogurt, and fresh baked pastries. Lunch choices include a ploughman's sandwich of Stilton cheese on a crusty roll with pickled onions, Cornish pasties, sausage rolls, and English finger sandwiches. And then there's high tea, totally civilized and satisfying. The scones, jams, cakes, and sherry trifle are quite good. From inside, the warm sunshine streaming through the windows is the only giveaway that you are in California and not in jolly olde England.

San Luis Obispo

Hotel/Bed and Breakfast Kissing

SYCAMORE MINERAL SPRINGS, San Luis Obispo
1215 Avila Beach Drive
(805) 595-7302, (800) 234-5831
Moderate

Call for directions.

Some people seem to live their lives in Jacuzzis. For them, a romantic getaway wouldn't be the same without one. And contrary to popular belief, this love of soaking in churning hot water isn't just a California phenomenon, it has become practically universal. While Sycamore Mineral Springs is every inch a California-style getaway, it is also a mecca for vacationers with tired, city-weary muscles or backs. The grounds are immaculate; large, well-maintained cedar whirlpool spas dot a beautiful wooded hillside that you approach from a steep, winding footpath. For $10 an hour you can reserve one for yourselves and soak to your hearts' content. You will be as revitalized, relaxed, and connected with nature as you could hope for. Well, almost. Although the brochure says "secluded," do not expect to be unseen by the other hot-tub lovers here. Also, be sure to ask for a spot that doesn't overlook the busy road below. Depending on your hot-tub needs, this place could be heaven on earth or a journey into California dreaming.

◆   **Romantic Note:** If privacy and a steamy dip are what you're longing for, a handful of efficient, motel-like rooms with their own large, private hot tubs are available. The units have been renovated but the fiberglass hot tubs are still not in the best shape.

Pismo Beach

Hotel/Bed and Breakfast Kissing

**SEA VENTURE HOTEL
AND RESTAURANT, Pismo Beach**
100 Ocean View Avenue
(805) 773-4994
Inexpensive to Very Expensive

From Highway 1, turn west on Ocean View Avenue to the hotel.

No one in their right mind would call the Pismo Beach area a romantic destination. Almost every street and shore is lined with motel-style accommodations in a variety of sizes, shapes, and price ranges. These are not wonderful locations for sharing precious time together, but the beachfront properties showcase the view, which is exquisite, at least off-season when it isn't obstructed by crowds of kids and hordes of beach enthusiasts. Off-season is the time to be here, early in the week, November to March, when you can walk forever on the expansive beach and feel like you own it.

The Sea Venture is, for the most part, just one of the handful of nice hotels that line the shore, with a few differences that make it special. Each room is very comfortable and attractive, and some have decks with private hot tubs that overlook the ocean. Now that's what I call romantic! There's also a lovely rooftop restaurant that has a wraparound view of the glorious passage of day into night. The food is quite good, although it can't really compete with the sunset. Still, this is one of the better places in the area for a meal, so don't miss it.

Solvang

Hotel/Bed and Breakfast Kissing

THE ALISAL, Solvang
1054 Alisal Road
(805) 688-6411
Unbelievably Expensive (includes breakfast and dinner)

From Highway 101, 40 miles north of Santa Barbara, take the Alisal Road turnoff west to The Alisal.

If you could take all of the things you don't like about tourist attractions and put them all together in one spot, it would most likely resemble the monotonous, banal town of Solvang. The Danish motif of every storefront is cliched and all-pervasive. There must be more than 200 businesses here thriving on busloads and carloads of tourists caught up in Nordic mania. But enough Solvang-bashing. This entry is about The Alisal. If not for this classic, contemporary dude ranch, you would have no reason to travel through or near the aforementioned tourist trap. Once you arrive at The Alisal, you will never want to leave, and because of the two meals a day and all the activities that come with your reservation package, you never have to.

The Alisal Ranch brings alive the idea of riding off into the sunset. Energetic horses take you over pastoral hillsides, alongside babbling streams and mountain lakes, and across rugged terrain (there are more than 10,000 acres of wilderness here).

The rooms vary from exquisite to ordinary, but even the basic bungalows are comfortable and surprisingly private. The pool and dining room are surrounded by immaculate grounds and ancient syc-amores (*alisal*, in Spanish) that gently bow in the wind. Every imagin-able diversion is available here: golf, windsurfing, sailing, fishing, lawn games, moonlight hayrides, outdoor barbecues, and tennis, to mention a few. For romantic purposes, a twilight ride should be foremost on your list. A kiss on horseback, with the colors of dusk setting the valley on fire, will be more elevated than you ever thought possible.

◆   **Romantic Warning**: Families flock to The Alisal during spring break, winter vacation, and summer recess. A more peaceful time to come here is when the kids are in school.

Ballard

Hotel/Bed and Breakfast Kissing

THE BALLARD INN, Ballard
2436 Baseline
(805) 688-7770
Expensive to Very Expensive

Call for directions.

Out in the middle of the rolling valleys of the Central Coast wine country, bordered by the majestic Santa Ynez Mountains and gracious vineyards, this stunning bed and breakfast provides a fabulous place for a snuggling, leisurely escape. A white picket fence frames the front of the building, with its old-fashioned veranda. Inside, the entrance and dining room are warmed by a huge wood-burning fireplace. Upstairs, the 15 inviting guest rooms are all outfitted in varying styles of authentic Americana. Affectionate, handsome details abound, including wood-burning fireplaces, antiques, wonderful quilts, and cozy sitting areas.

Downstairs, the expansive living room, warmed by yet another fireplace, is the site of generous, delectable afternoon wine tastings, complete with hot and cold hors d'oeuvres, quiche, chicken skewers, and crab dip. In the morning, enjoy a formal, gourmet breakfast at a linen-covered table for two in the charming dining room. The tantalizing menu includes such choices as eggs benedict with a perfect hollandaise sauce; a Danish omelet with jack cheese, sausage, and mushrooms; or a feather-light waffle with real maple syrup. All of the fresh pastries are a taste delight.

Most people are tempted to stay in the Santa Barbara area when visiting this part of the Central Coast. Do yourselves a favor and consider this less-crowded, tranquil town. A few days at the Ballard Inn will help you rediscover what the words "serene" and "calm" really mean.

◆ **Romantic Suggestion**: Across the street from the Ballard Inn is **THE BALLARD STORE RESTAURANT AND BAR**, 2449 Baseline Avenue, Ballard, (805) 688-5319, (Inexpensive to Moderate). This well-known restaurant serves a remarkable array of international dishes that are beautifully prepared and relatively inexpensive. The setting is lovely and the location remote. Most evenings the menu includes a prix-fixe dinner (an unbelievable $15.50 per person) that may present artichoke hearts baked with garlic butter and cheese, a rich fresh bouillabaisse, and a decadent dessert tray. You can also order a gourmet picnic basket, in advance, for a perfect afternoon outing. Fresh fruit and cheeses, half of a roasted chicken, French bread, and choco-late-chestnut mousse are part of one selection. The wine country, The Ballard Inn, and The Ballard Store Restaurant are all conducive to a perfect city escape.

Los Olivos

Hotel Bed and Breakfast Kissing

THE GRAND HOTEL, Los Olivos
2860 Grand Avenue
(805) 688-7788, (800) 446-2455
Expensive to Unbelievably Expensive

From Highway 101 exit onto Highway 154 heading to Los Olivos. Turn left onto Grand Avenue and go two blocks to the hotel.

The small (and I mean small) town of Los Olivos is flanked by abundant vineyards and the rugged Santa Ynez Mountains. In the heart of all this outdoor beauty is the luxurious, stately Grand Hotel. You will find nothing rustic inside here: everything from the furnishings to the service displays polish and sophistication. For the most part the rooms feel more like a hotel than a country inn, but they are spacious, with attractive detailing such as beamed ceilings, fireplaces, down comforters, and tile bathrooms. A bottle of local wine awaits your arrival and continental breakfast is delivered to your room in the morning.

The Grand Hotel is also home to an elegant, attractive restaurant called **REMINGTON'S**. Breakfast, lunch, and dinner become special occasions as you begin or end a day of touring the wineries. The eclectic menu is a potpourri of cuisines, with an emphasis on California and touches of Cajun and Thai.

Outdoor Kissing

WINE TOURING

From Santa Barbara, head north on Highway 154 to Highway 246 and turn left. The first winery you come to is Gainey Winery, near the town of Santa Ynez.

The majestic Santa Ynez Mountains and valleys are home to a fair number of wineries trying vigorously to compete with their Northern California cousins. If you've toured the Napa and Sonoma wine country, these vineyards are likely to be a disappointment. After all, the northern counties were left alone and allowed to flourish during Prohibition, while the southern territory was literally axed into submission. This rich, verdant land, kissed by the sun and perfectly cooled by ocean breezes, has laid fallow until just recently. The Southern California resurgence of enology is as promising as it is intriguing. If you have a penchant for tasting young wines with a distinct personality, then a day trip through this select countryside is more than worth the time and trouble. What can that do for your amorous dispositions? If the scenery doesn't evoke heightened emotions, a picnic at one of these beautiful, inspiring wineries will.

The most visually stirring vineyards in the area are **BYRON VINE-YARDS**, 5230 Tepusquet Road, Santa Maria, (805) 937-7288; **GAINEY**

VINEYARD, 3950 East Highway 246, Santa Ynez, (805) 688-0558; SANFORD WINERY, 7250 Santa Rosa Road, Buellton, (805) 688-3300; and ZACA MESA, 6905 Foxen Canyon Road, Los Olivos, (805) 688-3310. These wineries are in picturesque settings embraced by the mountains and blessed with penetrating views. The outdoor seating is where some potent afternoon memories can be fomented (which should not be confused with fermented).

◆ Romantic Note: There is actually abundant wine touring throughout the Southland. An excellent guide to the various wineries, lodgings, and restaurants is *The Wine Spectator's Wine Country Guide To California*, available by mail from: 601 Van Ness Avenue, Suite 2014, San Francisco, California 94102, (415) 673-2040. This magazine lays out the territory quite clearly, without affectation or hoopla. Just honest information for wine connoisseurs with some Gypsy in their soul.

◆ Romantic Suggestion: Along the backroads, nestled in a lush vineyard setting, is a rustic, exceptionally pretty white frame structure called MATTEI'S TAVERN, Highway 154, Los Olivos, (805) 688-4820, (Moderate). There is little about this place you won't find aesthetically suitable for a quiet afternoon or early evening interlude. Wineries and hillsides surround the outdoor patio. Inside, wood floors, a massive stone fireplace, lace-shaded windows, and well-spaced tables are just as inviting. The food is country-fresh American—not fancy, just very good.

Santa Barbara

Santa Barbara has been widely praised. Words like "idyllic," " heavenly," " flawless," and "irresistible" crop up regularly, and more than one travel expert has referred to it as California's own Shangri-la. Those who have visited this oceanside mecca know that those superlatives are not far from the truth. Against all odds, Santa Barbara has remained small enough to be picturesque and yet is large enough to please the most finicky urban sophisticates. It combines the moneyed influence of Los Angeles' upper echelon with the nonchalant, lackadaisical attitude of the young and those who think it's still 1968. In the elegant haute-couture boutiques, the funky hangout-type restaurants, and the entertaining fashion statements that stroll along the beach, you can observe the coexistence of very different life-styles. Regardless of where you choose to fit in, almost every building, park, promenade, and view is radiant, desirable, and unbelievably romantic. Satisfy your own curiosity and take the time and effort to discover this place for yourselves. Yes, it gets crowded. The exodus from Los Angeles northward on weekends can be, to say the least, arresting. But once you arrive and settle down, the masses will seem to disperse and all you will concentrate on are the blue waters of the Pacific, the undulating profile of the Santa Ynez Mountains, and the carefree sounds of your own laughter and joy.

◆ **Romantic Note:** Santa Barbara has something for everyone: wineries, hikes, whale watching, tennis, bicycling, flea markets, antique shops, museums, windsurfing, scuba diving, island excursions, and sightseeing attractions. To become more familiar with all the physical and aesthetic opportunities available, stop at the **VISITORS INFORMATION CENTER**, located at the corner of Cabrillo Boulevard and Santa Barbara Street, (805) 965-3021, for help with your personal itinerary.

◆ **Second Romantic Note:** One of the primary reasons to visit the Santa Barbara area is to spend hours luxuriating at the beach, basking in the sun's glory and feeling the sand slide beneath your feet. To avoid the crowds who also want to wallow in this Pacific Coast beauty and warmth, drive north from town on Highway 101 and look for the handful of signs that point the way to off-the-beaten-path beaches. To reach **MESA LANE BEACH**, follow Cliff Street to Mesa Lane where it dead-ends at the beach. **GAVIOTA BEACH** is located off Highway 101, a few miles south of Gaviota. **REFUGIO STATE BEACH** is in Goleta, just off Highway 101. You won't be entirely alone, and during July and August nothing out here is really a secret, but these beaches won't be quite as intensely populated as the oceanfront walk along Cabrillo Boulevard in the heart of Santa Barbara.

Hotel/Bed and Breakfast Kissing

THE BAYBERRY INN, Santa Barbara

111 West Valerio
(805) 682-3199
Inexpensive to Moderate

At the corner of Valerio and Chapala streets.

   If you expect endearing country finery or spacious, rustic interiors with contemporary enhancements when you stay at a bed and breakfast, then The Bayberry Inn might be a disappointment. Not that it isn't beautiful and brilliantly put together, because it is. But if you're not turned on by French furnishings and effects from the period of Louis XIV through Louis XVI, you won't be turned on by The Bayberry either. The owners have obviously been greatly impressed by the palaces of Versailles and Trianon. All eight rooms, including the guest suites, the gracious living room, and the royal dining room, are decorated with many of the same regal appointments and furnishings. The ceilings are draped in yards of satin, neatly pleated around small crystal chandeliers that reflect prismatic rose-colored light throughout the inn. The canopied beds enjoy this same overhead artistry. Luxurious down quilts, fireplaces, tiled bathrooms, and sitting areas are some of the comforts provided. The breakfasts are elaborate and the outdoor patio is a wonderful setting in which to enjoy The Bayberry Inn's gourmet morning meal, one of the best you'll enjoy anywhere. If pomp and circumstance are what your hearts desire, this is the place for you.

   ◆ **Romantic Note:** The Bayberry Inn is located near the heart of downtown Santa Barbara. The location is convenient but the street can be very busy at rush hour.

BLUE QUAIL INN, Santa Barbara
1908 Bath Street
(805) 687-2300, (800) 549-1622 (California),
(800) 676-1622 (elsewhere in the U.S.)
Inexpensive to Expensive

Call for directions.

This meandering bed and breakfast offers nine eclectic guest rooms. Two of the rooms are in the main house, four are located in a bungalow in the backyard, two more are in a small house next door, and one is a completely private cottage. Each of the rooms is decorated in an interesting assortment of second-hand furnishings mixed with antiques and winsome details. Some rooms have private baths, others share facilities.

Every evening wine and hors d'oeuvres are followed by a late-night sampling of sweets and apple cider in the main living room. Breakfast in the morning is often served on the garden patio under generous shade trees. Unfortunately, an apartment building just beyond the fence overshadows the potential for a country feeling in this setting. But the overall ambience is pleasant and the hospitality gracious.

THE CHESHIRE CAT, Santa Barbara
36 West Valerio Street
(805) 569-1610
Moderate to Expensive

At the corner of West Valerio and Chapala streets.

I know this may sound like an exaggeration, but every room at this bed and breakfast is charming, intriguingly romantic, beautifully decorated, and filled to the brim with heart-tugging ambience. Many of the 12 suites have a private Jacuzzi bath, fireplace, private patio, high ceilings, attractive sitting room, and large, wood-frame, beveled windows that let the sunshine stream inside. The colors and furnishings throughout The Cheshire Cat can only be described as creative. If the weather cooperates, a continental breakfast is served on the tiled garden patio, where tables draped in pink linen are bordered by flowers and a white-trellised gazebo.

By the way, in keeping with the inn's name, all the room labels are extracted from *Alice in Wonderland*. Don't let that cute quirk worry you; it is the only eccentric nuance you will find here. Everything else is Victorian elegance and plush comfort.

◆ **Romantic Warning:** Don't expect hands-on attention from the innkeepers; this is not that kind of bed and breakfast. You are pretty much on your own here, which can be preferable for those looking for privacy.

EL ENCANTO, Santa Barbara
1900 Lausen Road
(805) 687-5000, (800) 346-7039
Inexpensive to Unbelievably Expensive

From Highway 101, exit onto Mission Street East. Follow Mission Street to Laguna Street, turning left past the mission. When the road divides, bear right and follow the signs to the hotel.

Whenever I asked someone what they considered to be the most romantic place in Santa Barbara, inevitably the name El Encanto came up. I don't always consider that to be a good sign. Quite often such popularity makes a place more crowded and noisy than romantic. Nothing could have been further from the truth about El Encanto. This venerable network of bungalows nestled in the hills soaring above the immaculate Mediterranean-like landscape of glistening blue ocean, mountains, and the neatly outlined streets of Santa Barbara is dazzling. Each extremely private unit, arranged in a sweeping garden landscape, is marvelously unique, ranging in style from the ultimate in plush interiors to the basic comforts of country living. El Encanto is a loving, graceful reminder of genteel living, exceptionally beautiful without being pretentious or formidable. When you drive up the winding road that takes you to the outskirts of town, you will feel that something special awaits you at the end.

◆ **Romantic Note:** The restaurant and lounge at El Encanto are indisputably the best in Santa Barbara from which to watch the sunset.

From this vantage point, the convergence of day and night creates torrid colors that seem to set the world on fire. On the outdoor terrace, the ocean breeze gently swirls around you, cooling the sun's blush from your cheeks—a cause for celebration any time of year.

FOUR SEASONS BILTMORE, Santa Barbara
1260 Channel Drive
(805) 969-2261
Unbelievably Expensive and Beyond

From Highway 101, take the Olive Mill Road exit west to Channel Road and turn north to the hotel's entrance.

The Four Seasons Biltmore deserves mention for its superb styling and genteel, gracious service. This is a four-star hotel with an eight-star mentality. Everything about this immense resort is gilt-edged, grand, efficient, and slick. The property, once a preeminent oceanside estate, was left practically intact when it was refurbished to its present stature.

The baronial Spanish-tiled lobby area flows effortlessly into the Biltmore's two stunning restaurants, **LA MARINA** and the glass-enclosed **PATIO**. The exquisite location—in an elite neighborhood, across the street from the ocean—provides magical views from **LA SALA LOUNGE** and a few select rooms. Many of the guest suites are traditional and hotel-like, with fairly stiff rates. A series of suites in the Beyond Belief price range are decorated in beyond-belief fashion.

If your expense account can handle the dent, this stunning hotel is probably best for conventions and business meetings. The Biltmore isn't exactly cuddly, but if your tastes run toward impeccable service, luxurious surroundings, and lavish detailing, you'll find it to be unsurpassed in the entire Santa Barbara area.

◆   **Romantic Note:** There is a private waterfront nightclub, health club, and Olympic-size pool complex across the street from the Biltmore. If you are a guest at the hotel, you have full membership privileges during your stay. In all my traveling and research, this is one of the most exceptional hotel amenities I have ever discovered.

THE GLENBOROUGH INN, Santa Barbara
1327 Bath Street
(805) 966-0589
Inexpensive to Expensive

On Bath Street, between Sola and Victoria streets.

Don't let the absence of a kiss rating dissuade you from considering this potentially precious place to stay. I say "potentially" because The Glenborough Inn has changed management and from the look of things they will get this place in heartwarming shape in no time at all. There are five rooms in the main house and four rooms in an 1880s cottage across the street. As the refurbishing continues you will find rich country fabrics and linens, down comforters, and antiques inside every room. Outside, a well-tended garden with a private hot tub is a wonderful setting for breakfast in the morning or wine and hors d'oeuvres in the evening. From all appearances this could be a four-lip place to stay.

THE OLD YACHT CLUB INN, Santa Barbara
431 Corona Del Mar Drive
(805) 962-1277, (800) 549-1676 (California),
(800) 676-1676 (elsewhere in the U.S.)
Inexpensive to Moderate

From Highway 101 take the Cabrillo Boulevard exit and turn west onto Cabrillo. Just past the bird refuge is Corona Del Mar Drive, where you turn east. The inn is one block up on your right.

The ocean waterfront of Santa Barbara consists of a huge expanse of beach bordered by a tree-dotted stretch of lawn that runs parallel to Cabrillo Boulevard. Across the street is a collection of motels, super hotels, and restaurants that have some view in their favor; otherwise I'd call them tacky. Tucked around the corner from all this, on a residential street, is The Old Yacht Club Inn, which makes the waterfront a wonderful place to call home for a few days. This bed and breakfast is run like a taut ship. Everything is Victorian perfection and the rooms are as cozy and comfortable as you could want. One room even has a Jacuzzi tub. The breakfasts are famous in the area for their creativity and gourmet recipes. If proximity to the water is an important vacation ingredient for you and you want to avoid the sterile environment of Santa Barbara's motel row, then finding The Old Yacht Club will mean your ship has come in.

◆ **Romantic Note**: Three Saturdays a month the inn serves a superlative five-course meal.

SIMPSON HOUSE INN, Santa Barbara
121 East Arrellaga
(805) 963-7067, (800) 676-1280
Moderate to Very Expensive

On East Arrellaga, between Santa Barbara and Anacapa streets.

This stately bed and breakfast is shielded from its downtown Santa Barbara location by formidable sandstone walls that are camouflaged by tall hedges and a wrought-iron gateway. The Simpson House Inn, a stunningly renovated Victorian mansion, sits atop a one-acre knoll of manicured lawns and flowering gardens. Sprawling oaks and blossoming magnolias dot the grounds with country refinement from every perspective. Inside, the 10 rooms are adorned in varying combinations of teak floors, white wicker furniture, English lace, antiques, Oriental rugs, down comforters, fireplaces, and french doors that open onto private sitting areas. The sumptuous breakfast in the morning and wine and hors d'oeuvres in the evening are served on the vine-laced veranda overlooking the gardens. It is not hard to imagine yourselves sharing precious moments in this charming setting; it is only hard to leave it and return home.

TIFFANY INN, Santa Barbara
1323 De La Vina Street
(805) 963-2283
Inexpensive to Very Expensive

On De La Vina Street, between Victoria and Sola streets.

As the innkeeper took us on a tour of this lavishly renovated mansion, we sighed at each turn. Every room seemed a paradise and we wanted to stay in each of them. One had a massive fireplace in front of a bed covered in a thick down comforter; another had a private terrace, a balcony, a fireplace, and engaging views of the surrounding area. After we passed the bright living room filled with sunshine and floral prints, we were led outside past the tree-encircled patio where we were told breakfast would be served the next morning. Then back into the house and down a short hallway to our room. It was absolutely perfect, with a canopied brass bed, a wood-burning fireplace, a tiled sunken Jacuzzi, and a separate sitting area. The time spent here was exactly what we needed. We felt closer and more energized than we could have ever imagined.

THE UPHAM, Santa Barbara
1404 De La Vina Street
(805) 962-0058, (800) 727-0876
Moderate to Very Expensive

At the corner of De La Vina and Sola streets.

From the moment we entered the lobby of this Victorian hotel, we wanted to stay forever. Specifically, we wanted to stay in the lobby. The plush interior, country furnishings, wood-burning fireplace, small sitting areas, and an endearing breakfast corner that overlooked the gardens were all soothing and heartwarming. The exterior of the main building is surrounded by a wood-planked veranda, redwood timbers, and well-tended gardens. We hoped our room would look exactly the same.

We were escorted to our room along a path that meandered past manicured lawns and other guest cottages. Our suite was nice enough, with its canopied bed, wingback chairs, a mahogany armoire, and gas fireplace. But once our bags were unpacked we turned to each other and said, "Let's go back to the lobby and stay there!" There are 49 other rooms, and most are quite lovely. The gardens are wonderful. Everything about our stay at The Upham was pleasurable, but nothing quite matched the atmosphere of the lobby, where we thoroughly enjoyed the continental breakfast in the morning and wine and cheese in the late afternoon and evening.

VILLA ROSA, Santa Barbara
15 Chapala Street
(805) 966-0851
Inexpensive to Very Expensive

On Chapala Street, just off Cabrillo Boulevard.

There are many hotels and motels across the busy street from Santa Barbara's beachfront. None of these are places I would recommend for a romantic interlude, with the exception of Villa Rosa. The mission-style stucco inn with red tile roof looks a bit like an apartment building from the outside, but inside the contemporary furnishings are comfortable and inviting. A nicely maintained courtyard surrounds a built-in swimming pool. The 18 rooms come in various sizes and colors; some have views, all have private baths. Continental breakfast and wine and hors d'oeuvres are served in the gracious lobby.

Restaurant Kissing

ALLEGRO, Santa Barbara
920 De La Vina Street
(805) 965-6012
Expensive

On De La Vina Street between Canon and Carrillo.

Allegro serves some of the best Mediterannean/Italian cuisine in the area. This charming home-turned-restaurant is a pleasant haven where you can enjoy delectable pastas, fresh fish, and veal.

If you're a regular visitor to the Santa Barbara area, you may know that Allegro used to be called Norbert's. In its former incarnation, diners could enjoy a rapturous three-hour culinary extravaganza. Because the owner has stayed the same, once a month Allegro has a Norbert's night, when you can dine splendidly in an atmosphere of romance and elegance. Call for these rare specific dates.

BRIGITTE'S, Santa Barbara
1327 State Street
(805) 966-9676
Inexpensive to Moderate

On State Street, between Sola and Victoria streets.

Brigitte's is one of three extremely attractive, petite cafes, all within a few steps of each other, that serve some of the freshest and most ingeniously prepared lunches and dinners in Santa Barbara. Brigitte's is the smallest of the three, but the food makes this place a standout. The menu is a resourceful blend of French and California cuisine; prepare for gourmet euphoria. There are only a handful of tables here and it can seem a bit cramped, but at off-hours it almost feels like home.

CITRONELL RESTAURANT, Santa Barbara
901 Cabrillo Boulevard
(805) 963-0111
Expensive to Very Expensive

Citronell is located on the third floor of the Santa Barbara Inn.

There are many wonderful things you can say about this appealing restaurant with wraparound bay windows, hardwood floors, wicker chairs, and an enticing menu. Much praise is due to the tantalizing dishes the kitchen turns out consistently for lunch and dinner. The presentations are beautiful and every taste is a bite of heaven. However, another reason to frequent this French jewel is because of its dazzling view of the ocean. Regardless of the reason you come here, you won't be disappointed. Well, you might be disappointed with the service; the nights we were here, the staff was strained and confused. But the food, view, and atmosphere can excuse all.

DOWNEY'S, Santa Barbara
1305 State Street
(805) 966-5006
Expensive

On State Street, between Anapomu and Victoria.

Downey's is a bit more formal and the ambience a bit more serious than you'll find at Brigitte's. One of the few really gourmet American restaurants for miles around, Downey's is worth a visit just to see how romantic Yankee dining can be. The interior is becoming and modest, though the feeling is intimate. The food is always superb and the menu changes nightly. Lunch is served Tuesday through Friday, dinner Tuesday through Sunday.

LOUIE'S, Santa Barbara
1404 De La Vina, in the Upham Hotel
(805) 963-7003
Moderate to Expensive

On De La Vina, between Victoria and Sola.

This attractive, cozy restaurant is a shining example of how dining and romance can fuse in perfect harmony. The elongated dining room seems to glow with silky golden light, and the tables are covered in choice crystal and china. The menu is creative, the ingredients remarkably fresh, and the dishes skillfully presented. Though the name of this restaurant is not one I would choose for such an intimate location as this, that is hardly a problem worth mentioning. Forget I said anything, and make your reservation.

MAISON ROBERT'S
1325 State Street
(805) 962-1325
Moderate

On State Street, between Anapamu and Victoria.

Maison Robert's is a traditional French provincial restaurant, with aged brick walls, wicker-backed chairs, open hearth, linen-draped tables, and subtle lighting. The food is fresh and savory, the sauces as velvety and rich as you could imagine. When your mood requires a subdued, serene atmosphere with authentic, satisfying French cuisine, spend your time at Maison Robert's.

OYSTER'S, Santa Barbara
9 West Victoria Street
(805) 962-9888
Inexpensive to Moderate

On Victoria, just east of State Street.

I do not recommend Oyster's because of the crazy legend about oysters being an aphrodisiac. Quite the contrary. This is an intimate, sweet spot for lunch or dinner, with a simple but provocative menu that happens to include oysters. I hesitated at first to include this pretty outdoor dining setting, because I didn't want the name to confuse the intent. After all, this travel guide is about courting and affection, not lust. But then again, what's in a name? This restaurant could be called anything and that wouldn't change its desirablity as a place for a romantic interlude.

WINE CASK RESTAURANT
AND WINE BAR, Santa Barbara
813 Anacapa
(805) 966-9463
Moderate

On Anacapa, between Canon and Guerra.

Set in a slate courtyard, surrounded by small shops, the sleek, almost austere interior of the Wine Cask is the stage for delectable fresh food prepared by an adept kitchen staff. Inside, a large stone fireplace warms a room of white textured walls and wood-beamed ceilings etched with gold paint. Each table is individually spotlighted from above, giving the room a stately mood.

The restaurant is connected to a large wine store. Together they put on special wine tasting/dining events. These state-of-the-art evenings (including champagne and hors d'oeuvres) are not to be missed. Wine connoisseurs and novices alike can discover the best the wine country has to offer in a cordial, polished atmosphere.

Outdoor Kissing

CHANNEL ISLANDS
ISLAND PACKERS COMPANY
1867 Spinnaker Drive, Ventura
(805) 642-7688
Expensive

Directions to Island Packers Company. Take Route 101 to Ventura. Just south of Ventura take the Victoria Avenue exit south. Follow Victoria to Olivas Park Drive and turn west. Olivas Park Drive eventually becomes Spinnaker Drive.

The Channel Islands are an ecological preserve of enormous magnitude and productivity, a wilderness spectacle overflowing with perilous cliffs, windswept grasslands, and profoundly remote hiking trails with unparalleled vistas. You are almost certain to stumble upon rock-clad inlets, steep bluffs that lead to white sand beaches, and tide pools with a miraculous amount of marine life. These waters are a prime destination for those who wish to explore nature's vast range of aquatic creations. From the smallest sea anemones to Pacific gray whales, and everything in between, everything you see will overwhelm and delight you.

Island Packers is one of several tour companies that lead boating excursions to the Channel Islands, which lie 10 to 70 miles off the coast from Ventura. Depending on which tour you choose, you can expect a sedate cruise to a tranquil island inlet for serene nature walks and phenomenal snorkeling and swimming in the clear Pacific waters.

Some destinations along this wilderness chain are not for delicate individuals who are attached to their car phones and coiffed hairdos. A trek out here is for those with adventure in their hearts and a willingness to leave civilization far behind. By some standards, these volcanic islands might not seem a haven for romantic encounters. But once you embark on a voyage to these ancient marine terraces, the exhilaration of a sea landing and the resplendent, immaculate territory that rises before you will make you feel nothing less than rapturous.

◆   **Romantic Note:** Two of the islands have campsites where the only amenities available, including water, are the ones you pack in yourself.

WHALE WATCHING, Santa Barbara
Moderate

Several companies in the Santa Barbara area can take you on boat tours to witness the seasonal migration of the California gray whales. Do not miss the opportunity to share this splendid adventure with someone you love. These magnificent creatures have an immense lesson to share with humans, which can only be understood when you see them for yourselves. A few of the most frequently recommended companies are **WHALE WATCHING ON THE CONDOR,** (805) 963-3564; **CAPTAIN DON'S,** (805) 969-5217; and **DOLPHIN CRUISES,** (805) 962-2826.

Montecito

Hotel/Bed and Breakfast Kissing

SAN YSIDRO RANCH, Montecito
900 San Ysidro Lane
(805) 969-5046, (800) 368-6788
Very Expensive to Unbelievably Expensive

From Highway 101 take the San Ysidro Road exit east and follow the signs two miles to the ranch.

San Ysidro Ranch is a world-famous resort, located in the foothills above Montecito, that attracts the rich and famous and those who want to be near the rich and famous. This place is as distinguished and upper crust as it gets in this part of the world. The cozy, yet spacious cottages scattered over the ranch's extensive acreage are designed for the ultimate in privacy and distinctive living. Each dignified unit offers impressively designed interiors, massive stone fireplaces, and floor-to-ceiling french doors that lead to a private outdoor patio with a Jacuzzi built onto a wood deck. Everything about San Ysidro Ranch makes it premium kissing territory. Two devoted-to-each-other people can be as reclusive here as they choose. Continental breakfast is included with your stay.

◆ **Romantic Note: THE STONEHOUSE RESTAURANT** (Expensive) at San Ysidro Ranch is a handsome place for lunch or dinner. The food is good, though we were expecting great, and it wasn't quite as romantic as we had hoped for. It seemed obvious that people here were more interested in seeing who else of note was staying at this mountain enclave than they were in romance.

Restaurant Kissing

BERNADETTE'S, Montecito
1155 Coast Village Road
(805) 969-1456
Expensive to Very Expensive

Call for directions.

If you look up "cozy" in the dictionary, it might refer you to Bernadette's. This petite, authentically French restaurant has only a handful of tables in a trellised courtyard location. The chairs are covered in floral fabric, and the walls are a soft pink. The chef's creative, traditional, but light menu is the reason to make a reservation here. Every dish is a taste sensation. You can linger a long time over a dining achievement like this.

> *"Love does not consist of gazing at each other but in looking together in the same direction."*
> Antoine du Saint Exupery

"The greatest heroes are those whose names are written on our hearts."

Flavia

GREATER LOS ANGELES

Hotel/Bed and Breakfast Kissing

THE BILTMORE, Los Angeles
506 South Grand Street
(213) 624-1011
Very Expensive to Unbelievably Expensive

Take the Harbor Freeway to Sixth Avenue. Head east to Olive Street and turn left going back toward Fifth Avenue; you won't be able to miss it.

The Biltmore Hotel is as grand as any palace in Europe. This hotel's only drawback, perhaps, is its location in the heart of downtown Los Angeles. To some people, a stay in downtown Los Angeles is equivalent to a vacation in the midst of urban blight. Yet for those who can conquer their big-city apprehensions, a weekend here could seem like a holiday in an island utopia. You need wander no further than the **CHANDLER PAVILION** to take in outstanding live theater, and either of the Biltmore's restaurants will lavish you with outstanding meals: the sensational, thoroughly fascinating **BERNARD'S**, where dining is an art event and not just a meal, or the more casual, brightly lit main-floor **CAFE COURT.** Even if you only tour the giant gilded halls and stop briefly to sip a brandy in the lobby bar, the Biltmore is well worth the trek downtown.

CENTURY CITY INN, Los Angeles
10330 West Olympic Boulevard
(213) 553-1000, (800) 553-1005
Inexpensive to Moderate

On West Olympic Boulevard, near Beverly Glen and Century Park West.

The street location is not the best, and the rooms are really just hotel standard, but a few special features, plus the low cost, make this simple hotel pure pleasure. The rooms, furnished with wicker and rattan furniture, all have a petite but comfortable sitting area and a small whirlpool bathtub. Some rooms have a circular staircase that leads to a loft bedroom. In the morning a complimentary continental breakfast is delivered to your room. The street noise may bother you, but the amenities make this inn a good getaway in the Los Angeles area.

CENTURY PLAZA HOTEL TOWER, Century City
2025 Avenue of the Stars
(213) 551-3300
Expensive to Unbelievably Expensive

Just off Santa Monica Boulevard, turn south onto Avenue of the Stars to the hotel.

This hotel is really too large to warrant a listing as a bona fide kissing establishment. The massive office-like high rise houses more than 1,000 rooms, six restaurants, and several banquet rooms. There isn't anything here I would call cozy or affectionate. However, once you enter your room the sweeping, expansive views will make up for any romantic deficiency. Actually, the rooms are nicely appointed, including a rather sexy marble bathroom and comfortable furnishings. So ignore the size of the building and the somewhat impersonal feeling and escape to your room atop the world to enjoy a scintillating sunset and the twinkling display of city lights.

CHANNEL ROAD INN, Santa Monica
219 West Channel Road
(310) 459-1920
Moderate to Expensive

Take Highway 10 west to the Pacific Coast Highway and turn right. From the highway, go to the third stoplight and take a very sharp right, which will put you on West Channel Road, just past Ocean Park. The inn is one block up on the left side of the road.

There are bed and breakfasts... and then there is the Channel Road Inn. Quality of this caliber is hard to find in general, and when you add it to all the romantic touches you yearn for, you have one of the most wonderful getaways in Los Angeles. The 14 rooms are beautifully done with cushy firm beds, lush down comforters, simple but unusual private bathrooms, fetching color combinations, and large framed windows that have decent ocean views and are draped in billowy fabrics. This cleverly renovated mansion has an elegant, congenial atmosphere, and the earnestness of the innkeepers is felt and seen at every turn. After a long day of exploring the nearby Getty Museum, Santa Monica Pier, or Will Rogers State Historic Park, a soak in the inn's hillside spa will be a great finish to a perfect day. Waiting in your room when you return will be white robes, homemade cookies, fresh fruit, and flowers. Breakfast in the morning is a tempting array of croissants, breads, muffins, fruits and baked eggs.

CHECKERS HOTEL KEMPINSKI, Los Angeles
535 South Grand Avenue
(213) 624-0000
Very Expensive to Unbelievably Expensive

Between Fifth and Sixth streets in downtown Los Angeles.

Located in central downtown Los Angeles, this gracious hotel will impress you. The exterior is done in a striking Spanish motif. The rooms range from comfortable and relaxing to stately one- or two-bedroom suites; two luxury suites come with a fireplace, living room, bedroom, and dining area. All the hotel's amenities are first-class: afternoon tea service, full health and spa facilities, and exceptional room furnishings provide the ultimate in residential elegance. Checkers Hotel Kempinski is the only small luxury hotel located in the heart of downtown Los Angeles.

◆ **Romantic Note:** CHECKERS RESTAURANT provides an air of relaxation and tranquillity, with plenty of space between tables and booths. The American cuisine is surprisingly good. The hotel also offers free limousine service for guests to any central downtown business area, Monday through Friday from 7:30 A.M. to 9 A.M. Also, free transportation to and from the Los Angeles Music Center is available for diners at Checkers Restaurant.

THE CHESTERFIELD, Los Angeles
10320 West Olympic Boulevard
(213) 556-2777
Inexpensive to Expensive

Take Santa Monica Boulevard to Avenue of the Stars and turn south on Olympic Boulevard to the hotel.

The street location of this surprisingly warm and inviting hotel isn't the best, but once you walk inside the impressive interior will be more than enough to take your mind off the city. The Chesterfield is a one-of-a-kind kissing bargain. Each of the appealing rooms here is done in attractive floral fabrics, with light wood armoires and furnishings. The service is competent and polite. Even the **BUTLER'S GRILL** restaurant is a delightful spot for breakfast or lunch. It isn't fancy, and some of it may seem like only a pleasant hotel, but in Los Angeles, at these prices, this is quite a discovery.

HOTEL BEL AIR, Bel Air
701 Stone Canyon Road
(213) 472-1211
Unbelievably Expensive and Beyond

Take Sunset Boulevard west past Beverly Hills to Stone Canyon Road and turn right. The hotel is visible from this intersection.

I know I sound like I'm exaggerating, but if you can afford it, the Hotel Bel Air is probably the best place to kiss in the Los Angeles area. I'm not the first nor the last starry-eyed seeker of never-never land to rave about this luxury hotel. From the 11 acres of garden and forest primeval to the plush contemporary interior and the overindulgent service, every detail will make you forget that this is a hotel. Instead you will think you're living in a sumptuous fairy tale.

Each room is stunningly decorated with luxurious furnishings, and many have wood-burning fireplaces, balconies, and private patios. Glass doors draped in soft billowy fabrics frame the entryways to some of the bungalow-like suites. Even the standard rooms are fairly plush and inviting, and the setting is really the best there is in the entire Los Angeles area. The dining rooms and lounge are formal and handsome, yet they also feel soft and inviting, as if being close and whispering sweet nothings were also part of the menu. A four-star experience by most standards; by ours, The Bel Air is a four-kiss extravaganza.

◆ **Romantic Note**: Hotel Bel Air is actually more affordable than you might think, at least in comparison to other posh hotels in the area, and it is infinitely more refined and charming. The setting alone is well worth the price. Double-check your holiday budget and consider making your escape to this intoxicating, luxurious place.

HOTEL SHANGRI-LA, Santa Moncia
1301 Ocean Avenue
(310) 394-2791
Moderate to Expensive

Take Highway 10 and exit, just before the highway dead-ends onto Fourth Street heading north. At Santa Monica Boulevard turn west to Ocean Avenue, where you turn north. One block down is the hotel.

If you're going to take full advantage of the Santa Monica area, you might as well stay for a couple of days. One of the prime Santa Monica locations is the Shangri-la, specifically its penthouse suite. This 1920s-style high rise faces Ocean Avenue, the major coast road through town. The suite has two nicely designed bedrooms, two baths, a living room, a kitchen, and a balcony that wraps around the entire hotel with a sublime view of everything. The hotel offers a continental breakfast and afternoon tea. At the Shangri-la you can have a thoroughly intimate weekend for two on top of the world. Those on a budget should look for another impetuous couple who might want to share the extra bedroom in this grand suite.

◆ **Romantic Note:** The other rooms in the hotel are nice enough but ordinary, with proportionately less view than the penthouse. The standard rooms are also proportionately less expensive.

◆ **Romantic Suggestion:** Around the corner from the Shangri-la is an enjoyable, intimate Greek restaurant called **SKORPIOS**, 109 Santa Monica Boulevard, (310) 393-9020, (Inexpensive to Moderate), where you can sip a demitasse and listen to the guitarist serenading you through an evening of loving conversation.

LA MAIDA HOUSE AND BUNGALOWS, North Hollywood

11159 La Maida Street
(818) 769-3857
Moderate to Very Expensive

Call for directions.

If I tell you that North Hollywood isn't romantic, it's much like telling you that the Pope is Catholic. In fact, if I told you otherwise you'd probably throw away this book. Well, what I want to say is that in the middle of unromantic North Hollywood there is a romantic oasis called La Maida House, the city equivalent of Fantasy Island for loving couples.

When you arrive, pretend that this 7,000-square-foot villa is your own private mansion. Wander through the many different sitting rooms and select your own personal nest. As at most bed and breakfasts, each room is decorated individually, but at La Maida House the 11 rooms have exceptional variations. The Cipresso Room is softly colored by stained glass windows that overlook the rose garden; the king-size bed is encircled by oversize wicker furniture. The Calla Room has its own Jacuzzi and a parlor area with a stone bay fireplace, beamed ceiling, and skylight for nighttime stargazing. The Giardino Room has its own garden and stained glass atrium, and the Portico Room has a Jacuzzi and a private flower-filled patio. I could describe the other rooms, or I could tantalize your palate by telling you about the gourmet country breakfasts (no animal products), but if you're not planning on staying here it would only cause you unnecessary suffering.

◆ **Romantic Note:** At your request, the innkeepers will prepare a truly grand four-course dinner, a picnic basket, or a pre-theater supper.

LOEW'S SANTA MONICA BEACH HOTEL,
Santa Monica
1700 Ocean Avenue
(310) 458-6700
Expensive to Unbelievably Expensive

From Los Angeles take the Santa Monica Freeway (I-10) west to the Fourth Street exit, turning right. One block down turn left on Colorado. Where Colorado ends turn left on Ocean. Two blocks down on your right is the hotel.

As one might expect of an oceanfront hotel of this size and status, the prices are high, the interior is posh and cavernous, and the service is exemplary, not to mention stuffy. But in a 350-room hotel anywhere, you might not expect to find guest rooms that are cozy, warm, and amenable to affection and relaxation. That's not to say there aren't business-type conveniences as well (after all, this is a hotel), but they are nicely tucked around oversize furnishings, thick comforters, and sand-colored fabrics and wall coverings. The most intimate rooms, regardless of what the concierge might tell you, are not the splendid, very expensive one-bedroom suites. There are a handful of ocean-view rooms that are a little larger then standard size and are simply gorgeous, plus they have balcony seating for two that is nothing less than spectacular.

The restaurant at Loew's is attractive, bright, very contemporary and large, with a glass-enclosed deck, which translates to unromantic. But the entire Santa Monica area is there for your discovery and enjoyment, and holds many romantic spots. You will be unequivocally pleased with your stay here, and will leave reluctantly.

◆ **Romantic Note:** The Sunday brunch buffet at Loew's is one of the most cornucopian and luscious I have ever seen. Be warned that after a feast of this dimension it will be difficult to kiss—or even breathe. The entire lobby is turned over to this extravaganza, which makes for a rather noisy Sunday morning.

MALIBU BEACH INN, Malibu
22878 Pacific Coast Highway
(310) 456-6444, (800) 4-MALIBU
Moderate to Expensive

On the Pacific Coast Highway, in the town of Malibu.

One thing you quickly learn as a travel writer is never to rely on the information you read in a hotel or bed-and-breakfast brochure. I wouldn't call the information misleading, but most of it is embellished and evasive. Still, every rule has its exceptions. The brochure for this inn says: "Inviting interiors are a Malibu Beach Inn trademark.... Each room is designed to create the feeling of being in one's own private cottage on the beach.... Each room has a private balcony above the beach that provides unparalleled views from Point Dume to Palos Verdes, perfect for watching an ever-changing ocean filled with sailboats, surfers, dolphins, and sunsets." That is all unquestionably true, and there is more. The interiors of each of the 47 rooms are attractive, with sliding glass doors that open to the surf just a few feet below, wood-beamed ceilings, tiled fireplaces, and hand-painted tile bathrooms. The brochure could add a paragraph or two about the scintillating sunsets, white sand beach, or the tiled oceanfront lobby, but the management must have known one picture, like one kiss, is worth a thousand words.

◆ **Romantic Alternative**: **MALIBU COUNTRY INN**, 6506 Westward Beach Road, Malibu, (310) 457-9622, (Moderate to Expensive), situated just off the main highway, high on a bluff overlooking the Malibu countryside, is a plain little motel-like bed and breakfast with 16 rooms, close to the beaches and mountains. Its location is superior and its rooms are decent and sweet (number 17, with a view and a fireplace, and number 16, with a large private deck and full ocean view, are the best), with plenty of solitude. It's not perfection, but it is Malibu and the price is more than reasonable, which makes it a kissing bargain.

LE BEL AGE, West Hollywood
1020 North San Vicente Boulevard
(213) 854-1111
Unbelievably Expensive

On North San Vicente Boulevard, just south of Sunset Boulevard.

Le Bel Age tries very hard to be a formal luxury hotel and in some regards it succeeds, but essentially it is a very nice, slightly pretentious hotel. The lobby and hallways are decorated with interesting pieces of original artwork. From the rooftop sculpture garden (which is lovely) and pool with sweeping vistas of the city below, to the vine-trellised courtyard filled with massive, modern wood carvings, there is much to appreciate beside the accommodations. The guest suites are spacious, more like apartments than hotel rooms. Each room is attractively appointed with a marble bathroom, soft lighting, and a bedroom area separated from the parlor by a raised platform with a wrought-iron banister or by an entirely separate room.

If a culinary tour de force is part of your romantic itinerary, you would do well to have dinner at Le Bel Age's **DIAGHILEV** restaurant. This ultra-expensive, ultra-posh dining room serves a unique blend of French and Russian cuisine that is sheer perfection. Soft classical music, deftly played on a harp and grand piano, creates a softly poignant atmosphere for the entire evening. But the food is the true seducer here, so be prepared.

The more casual **BRASSERIE RESTAURANT** is a pleasant place to meet for breakfast before exploring the city at large or for jazz in the evening. I have to admit, in spite of the hotel qualities, I was delighted with Le Bel Age for the location, the conveniences, and the style.

◆ **Romantic Note:** The less-expensive rooms are actually the most appealing at Le Bel Age. The standard rooms have a bedroom separated by an elevation change from the living room and are simply precious. The mini-apartment suites, where the bedroom is a separate chamber from the living room, are a bit sterile for my taste. If you don't require a private meeting area and the room is only for the two of you, you'd be better off with a standard room.

LE VALADON, West Hollywood   ❤❤❤
900 Hammond Street
(310) 855-1115, (800) 776-0666
Moderate to Very Expensive

Take Sunset Boulevard one block past Doheny to Hammond Street and turn right to the hotel.

From the outside Le Valadon looks like an urbane, residential apartment building. From the inside it is an attractive, well-run hotel, with amenities that make it one of the better places to stay in greater Los Angeles. Each of the spacious rooms has a gas-burning fireplace, settee, and tile bathroom with a large glass-enclosed shower. Up on the roof you will find a wonderful swimming pool and whirlpool spa with sweeping, unobstructed views of the entire area. The rooftop tennis court enjoys the same vista. A charming, petite restaurant on the main floor serves relaxing breakfasts and intimate lunches and dinners. The food is surprisingly good, but the atmosphere and privacy are even better.

THE MANSION INN, Marina Del Rey   ❤
327 Washington Boulevard
(213) 821-2557, (800) 828-0688
Inexpensive to Moderate

Call for directions.

The name is a bit artificial, so don't expect this inn to be a mansion of any kind. What you can expect is a simple, congenial bed and breakfast. The rooms have comfortable furnishings, but all in all are a bit too much on the motel side of things to be considered a romantic getaway. The Mansion Inn is, however, one of the few really nice places to stay near the beach. For location, price, and homey extras like the continental breakfast served on the cobblestone courtyard every morning, it is a pleasing place to stay.

THE PENINSULA, Beverly Hills
9882 Santa Monica Boulevard
(213) 273-4888, (800) 462-7899
Unbelievably Expensive

On Santa Monica Boulevard, just west of Wilshire Boulevard.

In the heart of Beverly Hills, this extremely refined, stunning hotel is clearly a bastion for the local and international powers of the movie industry. Without question, this is the ultimate in deluxe hotel accommodations. Every floor has its own private valet and each room has its own call button to summon their services. Most rooms are designed to favor the pursuit of business, with private fax machines and phones everywhere you look. There is even a Rolls Royce available for complimentary service to Rodeo Drive and Century City, or you can rent it by the hour if you want to go off on a tour of your own. The list of amenities goes on and on. All of the rooms are beautiful and the bathrooms are appropriately sleek and sexy. However, the coveted guest locations are the private-entrance villas. Garden pathways lead you to these lavish accommodations, with private terraces, spas, and fireplaces. Sigh. You can't get much more majestic than this.

The hotel's **BELVEDERE** restaurant would be enchanting for almost any meal, but romance is not foremost on anyone's mind here. This is a deal-making restaurant—from the appetizer of Sonoma foie gras in black mushroom aspic to the entree of baked sole in a herb brioche crust with chervil butter. However, many affectionate moments could be spent in the plush surroundings of **THE LIVING ROOM**, where a provincial high tea is served. The waitstaff can be slow to incompetent, but if you're not in a hurry (and you shouldn't be, for an afternoon of intimate conversation), the presentation is regal and the price more than reasonable. The Royal Tea includes Perrier Jouet champagne, fresh strawberries, pastries, scones, delicious tea sandwiches, and tea for $20 per person.

RADISSON BEL AIR SUMMIT, Brentwood
11461 Sunset Boulevard
(213) 476-6571
Moderate to Expensive

Take the San Diego Freeway to Sunset Boulevard. Go west on Sunset Boulevard to the hotel entrance.

For all intents and purposes, this is just another hotel, except for a series of newer rooms located up the hill from the main building. These suites are called "Vista Designer" rooms, and they are spacious, lavish, and thoroughly comfortable. The hotel provides a continental breakfast, which contributes to the atmosphere of bed-and-breakfast hospitality, yet there are all the little vacation amenities that only a large hotel can offer: swimming pool, lounge, restaurants, room service, and tennis courts. The Bel Air Summit has a complimentary chauffeur service to drive you to nearby Beverly Hills, Westwood, and Century City. Look past the hotel facade and find solace and passion in your own personal suite.

THE RITZ CARLTON, Marina Del Rey
4375 Admiralty Way
(310) 823-1700, (800) 241-3333
Expensive to Unbelievably Expensive

Call for directions.

Of all the hotel chains I have stayed at across the country and in Europe, the Ritz Carlton is perhaps the most consistent: you can anticipate careful attention to detail and service at every one, including this branch in Marina Del Rey. Expect to find the quality the Ritz Carlton is known for: rich, stately appointments and amenities, conscientious service, and somewhat aristocratic airs. Although the rooms are basically just very nice hotel rooms, they are nonetheless comfortable and quite handsome. The hotel also offers tennis courts, a swimming pool, and, of course, the view of the marina.

THE DINING ROOM and THE CAFE restaurants both provide ultra-expensive, regal dining experiences. THE LOBBY LOUNGE AND TERRACE is a sedate, plush spot for cocktails and high tea.

◆ **Romantic Alternative:** The **MARINA DEL REY HOTEL**, 13534 Bali Way, Marina Del Rey, (310) 301-1000, (Moderate to Expensive), is a very attractive hotel in the heart of the marina; most of the rooms look out over the harbor. The casual atmosphere has hints of elegance, the service is surprisingly good for a hotel this size, and the rooms are fairly spacious. The above-average standard hotel furnishings are very comfortable. Real finds here are the **CRYSTAL SEAHORSE** and **DOCKSIDE CAFE** restaurants. Both serve excellent California cuisine, and the harbor-view settings are elegant and serene.

THE REGENT BEVERLY WILSHIRE, Beverly Hills

9500 Wilshire Boulevard
(213) 275-5200
Unbelievably Expensive

At the intersection of Wilshire Boulevard and Rodeo Drive.

This is one of the sexiest hotels I have ever seen. At most big-name hotels, it's the lobby area or the restaurants that elicit acclaim; the guest rooms tend to be just nice, average hotel rooms. At the Regent, that is not the case. Even though the lobby is nice enough and the restaurants serve excellent food, their ambience is not the least bit intimate. In this prestigious hotel, the rooms—the lush, beautifully appointed guest suites—are where you want to be for a weekend with your special companion. You can embrace from here until eternity, or as long as you can afford the stiff room rates.

These oversize suites have overstuffed sofas and chairs, ultra-thick down comforters, special windows that let the light in but keep the noise out, and tall ceilings, but their most alluring feature may be the sensual bathrooms, the size of most hotel rooms. The marble floor and counters frame a bathtub built for two, a separate glass shower stall built for a small crowd, and a lovely vanity area for apres-bath primping. In addition, superb service is of paramount concern to the management.

ST. JAMES CLUB HOTEL, West Hollywood
8358 Sunset Boulevard
(213) 654-7100
Very Expensive to Unbelievably Expensive

On Sunset Boulevard at La Cienega.

The St. James Club Hotel is an exceedingly elite association with branches in London, Paris, and Antigua. It is also stately and ornate, and the fact that it's private only adds to the glamour. However, private doesn't mean you can't stay here. Members-only status is reserved for the restaurant and lounge; hotel guests also have dining privileges, so all you need is a reservation and a charge card with credit to spare.

From every perspective, inside and out, the St. James is very art deco. If you are not an aficionado of the '20s, you could find the interior a bit much, to say the least. If you are an art deco buff, you will find that the guest suites reflect the same attention to elegance and detail as the public areas, only with a more sensual appeal. The restaurant and lounge are actually too business-oriented for intimate dining—but then that's what room service is all about, isn't it? A weekend here, all by yourselves, can be magical.

THE VENICE BEACH HOUSE, Venice
15 30th Avenue
(310) 823-1966
Inexpensive to Moderate

Call for directions.

There are not many traditional bed and breakfasts close to Los Angeles, but the Venice Beach House is a surprising exception that blends nicely into the oceanfront community that surrounds it. The large blue-framed house is one very short block from the part of Venice

Beach that is not famous for its hordes of unclad roller skaters. The interior is simply and comfortably decorated, and most rooms are bright and attractive. I wouldn't call this place luxurious, even though one of the nine rooms has a Jacuzzi tub and another has a fireplace: it lacks polish and is in need of a quality renovation. Nevertheless, it is a respectable alternative to hotel accommodations—and the reasonable prices are hard to ignore. If beach property, a relaxing atmosphere, and hearty breakfasts served in a courtyard setting are high priorities for your heart and soul, The Venice Beach House will suit you.

Restaurant Kissing

ALICE'S RESTAURANT, Malibu
23000 Pacific Coast Highway
(310) 456-6646
Moderate

Directly off Pacific Coast Highway, on the west side of the street. Look for a large white building with a huge sign atop that proclaims you have arrived at Alice's.

If visions of the '60s entered your mind when you saw the name of this restaurant, let me assure you that nothing inside this quaint establishment will remind you of that unromantic era. You should also ignore the exterior of the building, an unimpressive massive white stucco structure that sits on the edge of the highway. But inside, you'll find beamed ceilings with rustic woodwork accenting an airy, pink-linened dining room that faces a wondrous view of the ocean—and I mean wondrous. Alice's also offers deck seating that allows you to walk hand-in-hand out to a terrace flanked by the Pacific Ocean. Alice's menu is one of the best on the coast, the food is remarkably fresh, and the dishes artfully prepared.

◆ **Romantic Alternative: SAND CASTLE RESTAURANT,** 28128 Pacific Coast Highway, Malibu, (310) 457-2503 (Moderate). This restaurant offers literal beachfront dining: not only does the dining room overlook the ocean, the entire building is actually on the beach.

Beachcombing or a stroll along the shore can easily precede or follow breakfast, lunch, or dinner. Do not expect intimate dining at the Sand Castle—popular dining maybe, but not intimate. Still, the setting, the view, and the somewhat cozy, all-American atmosphere make for a casual, knock-the-sand-off-your feet kind of interlude that is hard to come by in these parts. Be sure to bring a blanket, because after your meal or snack the two of you are going to want to engage in some sand encounters of the third kind.

BEAU RIVAGE, Malibu
26025 West Pacific Coast Highway
(310) 456-5733
Moderate to Expensive

Directly off Pacific Coast Highway, on the east side of the street.

This is a charming Mediterranean-style restaurant where the flower-filled patio surrounded by stone walls, a terra-cotta tiled floor, and wrought-iron furnishings hidden by foliage set a made-to-order romantic mood. Beau Rivage is particularly provocative for a Sunday brunch or early dinner. The sun-filled dining room that bears witness to the ocean's tidal comings and goings is a delight for tired hearts in need of an escape from the usual. Take your time; this is leisurely continental dining at its coastal romantic best. Dinner is served nightly, and brunch on Sunday.

BISTRO GARDENS, Beverly Hills
176 North Canon Drive
(213) 550-3900
Expensive

On Canon Drive, off Wilshire, two blocks east of Rodeo Drive.

In spite of its must-be-seen-in reputation, Bistro Gardens is a fine spot for a rendezvous anytime. Less stuffy than Citrus (and far easier to get into), and more spacious than Ma Maison, the Bistro offers the best of outdoor and indoor dining, Beverly Hills-style. The garden tables are decorated with pastel tablecloths and colored umbrellas surrounded by hanging flowers. The shaded lights, unusual flower arrangements, and flowing fountain create a lovely setting for lunch. After sundown the garden is lit from above by lights in the towering trees, and live classical piano music plays in the background. Inside the tables are intimate and surrounded by mirrors, antique lamps, and lavish centerpieces. The hardwood floors and marble bar add to the enchanting ambience. The food, continental with touches of spa cuisine, is really quite good—not great, but thoroughly satisfying.

◆   **Romantic Alternative**: A few steps away from the Bistro Gardens is the beautiful **BISTRO RESTAURANT**, 246 North Canon, Beverly Hills, (310) 273-5633, (Expensive to Very Expensive). Owned by the same proprietors, the Bistro Restaurant offers French cuisine in a dimly lit, lavishly decorated Beverly Hills relic. Inside, hand-painted columns are interspersed with elongated mirrors featuring hand-etched glass. This Parisian-style restaurant is often crowded at night and it can be a bit stuffy, but, well, this is Beverly Hills.

◆   **Romantic Suggestion**: A couple of blocks west of both Bistro restaurants lies a stretch of shops resembling a European street. **ONE RODEO**, at the corner of Wilshire Boulevard and Rodeo Drive, directly across from the Beverly Wilshire Hotel, is a short upward climb great for romantic strolling. The hill is paved in cobblestones; the shops look like gorgeous Italian architecture and are surrounded by flowing fountains.

BUTTERFIELD'S, West Hollywood
8426 Sunset Boulevard
(213) 656-3055
Moderate

One block east of La Cienega, on the south side of the street. Parking is located on Olive Street.

I told a friend of mine who also writes travel books that I thought Butterfield's was a very romantic restaurant and I was thinking of including it in this book. She had a hard time thinking of Butterfield's as a place that would meet the book's kissing criteria: for her it was a

neighborhood hangout and not a place she would go for tender inter-
ludes. I said that I thought the outdoor seating in a quiet garden setting
was charming and that the cottage-like interior of the main dining
room, adorned by a glowing fireplace, was appropriately cozy. I also
commented that the Sunset Boulevard address might make people
think that outdoor dining meant inhaling car fumes with their appetizer
and entree, but that Butterfield's secluded patio is set back far enough
from the street that patrons probably wouldn't even hear a car. We both
agreed that the food is good and reliable, not fancy but good, and the
prices more than reasonable for the area. I said I found all of that
fairly romantic. "Maybe it is," she conceded. "I guess that after a while,
when places become too familiar, you lose that kind of perspective." I
urged her to have another look. She agreed, and a week later I got her
report: "My date and I both thought it was a great kissing place. Thanks
for the 'new' recommendation!" Lunch and dinner are served seven
days a week.

CAFE DES ARTISTES, Hollywood
1534 North McCadden Place
(213) 461-6889
Moderate

*From Hollywood Boulevard, just past the Hollywood Roosevelt Hotel, turn
south on North McCadden Place.*

In a city known for its slick, chic interiors, Cafe des Artistes is like a
breath of fresh air for those in search of easygoing, rustic, genteel dining.
The rough-hewn country interior is modest and lovely. There are only
a handful of tables in the dining area; the bright patio seating is cloistered within abundant foliage that nevertheless permits the warmth of
the sun to shine through. You will find the same atmosphere and
delectable menu selections at either lunch or dinner. One warning: the
street location of Cafe des Artistes is best described as bleak or, as a
friend said, forbidding. Just hold hands tightly until you get inside and
then loosen your grip, stay close, and relish the evening ahead.

CAFE MONDRIAN AND LOUNGE, West Hollywood
8440 Sunset Boulevard
(213) 650-8999
Moderate to Expensive

Take La Cienega to Sunset and turn right. The Mondrian Hotel is one block down on your right. Watch for the driveway or you will easily pass this one by.

The Mondrian Hotel sits atop a bluff at the base of the Hollywood Hills, with a dramatic view of Los Angeles' endless promenade of lights. From the restaurant you can watch this scene through substantial floor-to-ceiling windows. The interior is an intense composite of black-and-white furnishings and fabrics in a sultry art deco style. In spite of all this high contrast, the mood is less formal than you might expect; an unconstrained atmosphere coexists winningly with a creative menu and talented kitchen staff. The cocktail lounge/piano bar has nightly entertainment and is separate from the dining room. Both spots can accommodate a successful beginning or a sentimental ending to a remarkable evening in Los Angeles.

CAMILLE'S, Sherman Oaks
13573 Ventura Boulevard
(818) 995-1660
Moderate to Expensive

On Ventura Boulevard, one block east of Woodman.

I know it's hard to believe, but you can find romance in the San Fernando Valley. Camille's makes sure that hearts and appetites are well taken care of and you don't have to cross the border (or traffic) into West Hollywood or Beverly Hills. The interior is somewhat old-fashioned but still very warm and inviting. The dining room, done in a rosy shade of pink, is filled with antiques, artwork, latticed hidden booths, and well-spaced tables. The dishes are very good and very French, and the prices are more than reasonable for the quality. You would do well to bring a date here—both of you will leave impressed.

CARLOS AND PEPE'S, Malibu
22706 Pacific Coast Highway
(213) 456-3105
Inexpensive

Take Highway 10 west toward Malibu; Highway 10 turns into Pacific Coast Highway at Santa Monica. Continue along this highway into Malibu and you will see a large red sign, indicating your arrival at Carlos and Pepe's.

For all intents and purposes Carlos and Pepe's is just like any other Mexican restaurant in the Los Angeles area, yet I can also say it is probably the most romantic. The generic accoutrements are all there: a large bar, hanging sombreros, and a terra-cotta floor. However, this restaurant is directly on the beach. Once past the bar, the lighting dims, tanks with exotic fish surround you, and you are seated 10 feet from the Malibu breakwater. It is the perfect place to dine after a day at the beach. The dress code is very casual, the prices very modest, and the view of the ocean breathtaking.

CASTAWAYS, Burbank
1250 Harvard Road
(818) 843-5013
Moderate

Call for directions.

I know it's hard to imagine that you can find romance in Burbank, but you can. Castaways has a remarkable setting—a panoramic view of the entire San Fernando Valley. The outdoor patio offers numerous tables with their own personal fireplaces. Inside, intimate booths and tables are crowned by hanging plants, beamed ceilings, and candlelight. The owners of The Reef own this place too. They know location, but not necessarily food, which is good, but not exciting or special. The bar, surrounded by glass and soft music, is the perfect place to ogle the magnificent view over an after-dinner drink together.

CHAMPAGNE, Century City
10506 Little Santa Monica
(213) 470-8446
Expensive to Very Expensive

Call for directions.

Champagne is not one those trendy restaurants Los Angeles is so famous for. But for those interested in exquisite country French cuisine served in a posh, unruffled, romantic atmosphere, it is a treasure. The menu features many tantalizing dishes. The roasted eggplant soup, terrine of wild pheasant and squab, sweet corn mousse, and wild mushroom and country green ragout in a hearty red wine sauce are fabulous. Count on a memorable evening.

CHEZ HELENE, Beverly Hills
267 South Beverly Drive
(213) 276-1558
Moderate

On Beverly Drive, between Olympic and Wilshire.

Even from the outside, Chez Helene looks like the perfect place for a leisurely, quiet evening or an afternoon of warm conversation and ambrosial dining. The thatched-roof brick home is located on the outskirts of the Rodeo Drive shopping district, surrounded by office buildings and bustling stores. This visual anomaly holds something very special inside. The casual interior looks friendly and quaint, with wood-beamed ceilings and hardwood floors. The small menu is authentically French and masterfully prepared; the service is congenial and relaxed. Take your time as you whisper sweet nothings, because no one here will hurry you along.

◆ **Romantic Alternative: COLETTE**, 9360 Wilshire Boulevard, Beverly Hills, (213) 273-1400, (Moderate to Expensive), is a charming, small restaurant inside the rather plain, almost austere Beverly Pavilion Hotel. Ignore the hotel and take a breather from the hectic pace of the city to unwind over an intriguing French menu, deftly prepared and beautifully served. Because of its hotel clientele, Colette opens daily at 7 A.M., which makes it one of the more intimate places to have an early-morning meal in Los Angeles. Sharing mornings like this can be habit-forming.

DAR MAGHREB RESTAURANT, Hollywood
7651 Sunset Boulevard
(213) 876-7651
Moderate to Expensive

On Sunset Boulevard, between Fairfax and La Brea.

Though at first this place may seem a bit too commercial and popular to be truly romantic—more special occasions are celebrated here than almost anyplace else in the city—something unbelievable happens when you wander into this traditional Moroccan restaurant. The aura is so enticing your skepticism will melt away and no one else in the restaurant will matter but the two of you. Feast on exotic food and visual delights, sink back into satiny pillows, let the seductive music soothe your city nerves, and allow yourselves to be pampered in a style once reserved for sheiks and caliphs.

DI STEPHANOS, Westwood Village
1076 Gayley Avenue
(310) 208-5117
Inexpensive

Between Weyburn and Kinross, in Westwood.

Westwood Village is UCLA territory, filled with bustling students and crowded movie houses. Amid this noisy, youthful atmosphere is a restaurant at odds with its surroundings. Hidden in the middle of Gayley Avenue, Di Stephanos, a family-owned restaurant, serves excellent traditional northern Italian food. Sinatra love songs and '40s jazz establish a romantic ambience. Each of the eight cozy booths is surrounded by antique etched mirrors and small rosebushes. A large wooden cupboard and flowered wallpaper give Di Stephanos a genial atmosphere, and the candelabras and antique ceiling fan providing a touch of elegance. Di Stephanos proves that not all romantic dining spots have to be pricey.

FLEUR DE VIN, Pasadena
70 South Raymond Street
(818) 795-0085
Expensive

On the corner of Green and South Raymond, in Old Town Pasadena.

Located across the street from the historic Castle Green building, Fleur de Vin is an intriguing combination of American casual dining and French elegance. Tapestries and original miniature paintings surround candlelit tables and a small, intimate bar, which, unfortunately, can get a bit crowded with the business crowd at cocktail hour. However, the order for any time of day is sublime French-California cuisine that is considered by some to be the best in the state. Your exquisitely presented dinner is accompanied by mellow live jazz in a softly lit, sleek dining room. This brasserie is a favorite dining spot for Pasadena residents for both lunch and dinner. The menu is updated every three months, and includes a superior prix fixe dinner at $39.95 per person.

THE FOUR OAKS CAFE, Bel Air
2181 Beverly Glen Boulevard
(213) 470-2265
Very Expensive

Take Sunset Boulevard to Beverly Glen Boulevard and turn north. The restaurant will appear suddenly on your left about four miles after you turn.

The Four Oaks is one of those ambitious, alluring dining productions Los Angeles is famous for. What makes this particular epicurean cafe an ardent spot for lunch or dinner is its Beverly Glen Canyon setting; you'll feel you've left the city far behind. The cottage-like home has been redone to reflect polished country refinement, and is surrounded by oak and eucalyptus trees. The petite rooms flow naturally, one into the other, though the tables are a tad too close for kissing comfort. Weather permitting, the outdoor patios are exceptionally lovely sites for dining. But what else would you expect in Bel Air? The food is a five-star celebration and the service efficient and knowledgeable.

GEOFFREY'S, Malibu
27400 Pacific Coast Highway
(310) 457-1519
Expensive to Very Expensive

Directly off Pacific Coast Highway, four and a half miles north of Pepperdine University, on the west side of the street. Watch for a large black-and-white sign above the restaurant and a small gray sign just before the driveway.

There is something sybaritic about sitting atop a towering cliff, perched over the ocean with nothing to do but watch the resplendent blue horizon, appreciate the person you're with, and receive service from a waiter who will attend to your every need. Geoffrey's offers all that and more; some of the "more" you could do without. I would call the food "Malibu fare" (the pancetta-and-gruyere frittata is perfect); the management calls it an eclectic, cross-cultural experience. Regardless, you can be seated at an outside table tucked between palm trees where you will feel the ocean mist caress your face as the two of you savor whatever the moment brings.

THE HOLLYWOOD ROOSEVELT
HOTEL'S LOBBY BAR, Hollywood
7000 Hollywood Boulevard
(213) 466-7000
Inexpensive

At the intersection of Hollywood Boulevard and La Brea Avenue, across from the old Grauman's Chinese Theatre.

Tourist traps are not romantic. Yet a trip to L.A. without touring Universal Studio, Disneyland, or the Spruce Goose, or taking a walk down star-paved Sunset Boulevard, is inconceivable. If you decide to go on the Sunset Boulevard stroll—which is a must at some time or another—and you need shelter from the pandemonium, stop in at the Lobby Bar at the Hollywood Roosevelt Hotel. The handsomely renovated interior with leather furnishings is a sight for sore sightseeing eyes. You can indulge in quiet thoughts and sweet discourse before once again braving the hordes outside.

◆ **Romantic Warning:** The hotel itself is nice, but the rooms are plain and mediocre, not what you would expect from a place that has undergone a costly renovation. A series of fairly outrageous suites are priced at more than $1,500 a night, but how many of us can kiss at those rates without choking?

◆ **Romantic Suggestion:** The **CINEGRILL LOUNGE** in the hotel is an attractive cabaret. Shades of mauve, black, and gray surround a small stage that hosts celebrity entertainment. Given the area, this evening spot is nothing less than an oasis in the midst of a desert.

IL CIELO, Beverly Hills
9018 Burton Way
(213) 276-9990
Moderate

On Burton Way, just off Doheny.

I was very excited when I discovered this Italian gem of a restaurant. Most of the pasta cafes I had encountered looked and felt aloof and redundant: good food, noisy cluttered atmosphere, tables lined up right next to each other, brusque service that left my stomach feeling fine and my emotions a bit jarred. For socializing that's great; for romance it's intolerable. Il Cielo is different. First of all, everything served was wonderfully fresh and hearty, and there were some very creative appetizer and pasta combinations. My confidence in the amorous potential of this place was given an added boost by the vine-cloaked patio, embroidered with trellises, flowering plants, and comfortable, intimate seating. Inside, wooden tables, a cobblestone floor, and a glowing fireplace made the interior as fetching as the exterior. A star-filled summer night would be well spent at this rare, inviting Italian cafe.

◆   **Romantic Warning:** The service can be a bit uneven, depending on the mood of your waitperson. It was hard to tell if our waiter was depressed that night or just disappointed that we weren't more worthy of his attention.

IL GIARDINO, Beverly Hills
9235 West Third Street
(213) 275-5444
Expensive

On the corner of West Third Street and Maple, three blocks west of Doheny.

While strolling through a residential area of Beverly Hills, I stumbled onto this small, hidden restaurant, its presence given away by a small canopy, a wicker bench, and a door encircled with ivy. The patio seating is limited to six tables with umbrellas, surrounded by potted geraniums along the sides. The inside tables are covered with colorful pink floral tablecloths and candles. The back room is decorated with bright pink-and-coral flowered wallpaper. Located in an out-of-the-way, secluded corner of Beverly Hills, Il Giardino provides the perfect spot for an intimate dinner in a part of town not known for subdued dining.

INN OF THE SEVENTH RAY, Topanga Canyon
128 Old Topanga Canyon Road
(310) 455-1311
Inexpensive to Moderate

You gain access to Old Topanga Canyon Road by following Topanga Canyon Boulevard north from Highway 1 or south from Highway 101. When you come to a small commercial area, turn west at the post office onto Old Topanga Canyon Road. The restaurant is almost immediately after the turn.

Inn of the Seventh Ray is one of those rare places where the physical setting and interior ambience are in perfect harmony. The restaurant seems to merge with the countryside. Set away from the road, next to a flowing creek, this rustic, unconventional building is approached from an area of Topanga Canyon that you wouldn't think of as enchanting; once you arrive, no other word will seem appropriate.

From the winding wooden stairway to the entrance, the building looks like a grand old church from the 19th century. As you walk around it and peer into the wood-framed windows, you'll see an eclectic collection of rustic rooms. Each dining area has vaulted wood-beamed ceilings and brick fireplaces that fill the room with golden warmth. A large outdoor seating area next to a creek looks out over the valley. Tall lamp heaters next to each table warm the cool night air when the temperature drops past the comfort zone. The inn serves gourmet health food that is simply delicious. The menu itself reads like a passionate love sonnet. You can easily slip into the mood that complements such a dining experience. Open for lunch and dinner seven days a week.

◆   **Romantic Note:** Although many vegetarian specialties are served, including organically raised produce, wines, herbs, and freshly baked breads, lamb, chicken, and steak dishes are also available.

J'ADORE, Palos Verdes Estates
724 Yarmouth Road
(213) 541-3316
Moderate

From Pacific Coast Highway, turn west onto Palos Verdes Drive West and then west again at Yarmouth Road. The restaurant is in a shopping strip area on the north side of the street.

When I met the very charismatic owner of J'Adore, I asked him about the name of his restaurant. "Shouldn't it be *je t'adore?*" I asked. In a pleasant French accent he replied, "*Non*, not at all. *Je t'adore* means 'I love you' and *j'adore* means 'I love it.' The difference is one of relationship. Here love has to do with the food and the sensations you get while dining. At that point, when your palate and feelings are heightened with good food and amiable surroundings, then you can more convincingly say 'I love you.'" His *tres* French attitude was fully reflected in his charming out-of-the-way restaurant, located in a small shopping area in

Palos Verdes Estates. The menu is outstanding and the care with which the dinners are prepared is evident in every bite. Wine tastings are held nightly and the menu changes frequently. The Palos Verdes area offers one of the more exquisite drives near the city, and a dinner here would finish your day beautifully.

LA CHAUMIERE, Century City
2055 Avenue of the Stars
(213) 277-2000
Expensive to Very Expensive

Located in the Century Plaza Hotel.

Romanesque murals in the elevator set the mood for your journey into this stunning dining experience. Rich wood paneling, a panoramic window display overlooking hills and garden, and a stately interior are all part of the production. The bar is warmed by a fireplace and filled with plush sofas and handsome leather-and-wood chairs. The food is usually impressive. Appetizers of duck liver in sweet port and figs, and salmon rolls in truffled bordeaux sauce were wonderful. Entrees of swordfish with black olive relish and pan-fried sea bass with parsley raviolis were also quite good. Between the setting and the menu, your appetite for romance and food will be more than satiated.

LA CONVERSATION, West Hollywood
638 North Doheny Drive
(310) 858-0950
Inexpensive

North Doheny is approximately one block north of Santa Monica Boulevard at Nemo.

This small cafe is the perfect place to enjoy a steaming cappuccino and a delectable fresh pastry while you share a few quiet moments together. There are only a handful of tables and the menu limited, but the setting is charming and the quiches, tortes, and sweets are excellent.

LA GRANGE, Westwood
2005 Westwood Boulevard
(310) 279-1060
Moderate

On Westwood Boulevard, between Pico and Little Santa Monica.

Situated in the heart of bustling Westwood is this unique French restaurant that resembles a rustic barn. Don't be misled: the only thing rustic here is the decor. The food and service are both extraordinary. La Grange's deep, comfortable leather booths are surrounded by country wood paneling decorated with farm items such as dried ears of corn, copper cookware, and hand-woven baskets. The beamed ceilings are filled with flowering plants hanging from the rafters and the windows are trimmed with lacy pull-back curtains. La Grange dishes up exceptional Parisian cuisine, at reasonable prices in a country paradise.

◆ **Romantic Note:** La Grange has special coupons offering dinner for two at $32.95, which includes an entree with vegetables, pate, soup or salad, a glass of wine, coffee, and dessert. Ask for a sample dinner menu and you will find the coupons on the back.

LE CHARDONNAY, West Hollywood
8284 Melrose Avenue
(213) 655-8880
Expensive

On Melrose, between Flores and Sweetzer.

Le Chardonnay is what a brasserie dining experience should be: charming, refined, casual, and very cosmopolitan. It is not inexpensive, though. In Paris a brasserie can be all those things and your wallet will not necessarily feel the impact. Nevertheless, at Le Chardonnay you can enjoy an afternoon or evening that is as relaxed as it is savory and congenial. The interior is a radiant combination of brass moldings, hand-painted tiles, carved wood detailing, mirrored walls, and an exposed cast-iron oven that sends flickers of firelight dancing across the glassy polished interior. The seating here is discreet, with tables and banquettes well spaced for intimate dining, and the service is polite. The food is excellent, at times phenomenal.

L'ESCOFFIER, Beverly Hills
9876 Wilshire Boulevard, in the Beverly Hilton Hotel
(213) 274-7777
Expensive to Very Expensive

On Wilshire Boulevard, near Santa Monica Boulevard.

After you make your way across the circular driveway of the Beverly Hilton Hotel, crowded with limousines and Rolls Royces, you will have a slight challenge in finding the correct elevator to whisk you up to L'Escoffier. This is where ballroom dancing (and a few novel variations on cheek-to-cheek twirling) is the primary if not sole focus of the evening. Some reviewers could grumble that the average couple on the dance floor is from the Charleston era, that the kitchen is in need of some professional help, and that the interior design straddles a fine line between opulence and kitsch. But from my perspective, when nothing else will do but honest, rhythmic, slow dancing that makes me feel like Ginger Rogers and him like Fred Astaire, then L'Escoffier is the ticket to a fantasy fulfilled. In spite of what the critics say, at night this place really does radiate with a golden, formal glow from every corner. And the live music is wonderfully traditional, with enough variety to satisfy every preference. Come here on a Monday, Tuesday, or Wednesday night and you may have the dance floor almost to yourselves.

◆ **Romantic Note:** If you want to avoid L'Escoffier's overpriced, mediocre menu, a handful of tables near the dance floor are available for cocktails and dancing.

◆ **Romantic Alternative: TOP OF THE HILLCREST**, 1224 South Beverwil Drive, in the Beverly Hillcrest Hotel, Beverly Hills, (213) 277-2800, (Moderate), is another starlight dance room that offers some arm-in-arm waltzing, with a preponderance of easy-listening pop disco. The tone and style of the restaurant are rather second-rate, and the entire hotel is in desperate need of a face-lift, but the floor-to-ceiling

windows all around the dining room are dramatic, the service is cour-
teous, and the menu is reasonably priced. If you like a tamer style and
less pretense than L.A.'s famous who's-who nightclubs, you can't do
better than here.

L'ORANGERIE, West Hollywood
903 North La Cienega Boulevard
(213) 652-9770
Very Expensive

On North La Cienega, near Romaine.

Los Angeles has a love affair with its French restaurants. The sheer
number of these lavish (or slick) dining rooms is mind-boggling. At first
glance, the task of making a decision among them may seem over-
whelming. But to devotees of haute cuisine and haute socializing only
a few elite selections are worth contemplating. The process is even
further simplified for those who are more concerned about the person
they're with than with the other people who may be there. If intimacy,
quiet conversation, words of love, and long gazes are important to you,
then L'Orangerie is one of those rare, popular places that is the essence
of romantic French dining.

You would be hard put to find a better French kitchen in all of
Southern California. The menu is intriguing and the dishes skillfully
and artistically prepared. If you find food seductive, be prepared to
swoon at every course. The interior might have the same effect on you.
When you enter you'll feel that you've arrived at a chateau somewhere
in the Loire Valley: tile floors, lofty ceilings, abundant foliage, arched
doorways, Louis XIV furnishings, and classical music playing in the
background. Unfortunately, the seating is fashionably tight and the
acoustics are tinny, but if you ask ahead of time for a special table, all of
this can be avoided.

LUNARIA, Santa Monica
10351 Santa Monica Boulevard
(310) 282- 8870
Expensive to Very Expensive

On Santa Monica Boulevard and Beverly Glen.

If you are in the mood to snuggle close to your dining companion, listen to some of the best live jazz in Los Angeles, and dine on luscious dishes, Lunaria is the place to frequent as often as you can get a reservation. At first glance you might mistake it for a trendy, overpriced Westside restaurant. However, the open kitchen, impressionist paintings, hand-painted dinner plates, rattan chairs, and cozy lighting create a serene, tender setting. After 10:00 P.M. the owners remove a partition between the jazz lounge and the main restaurant so that diners can linger after eating and view the performance.

◆ **Romantic Note:** If dinner at Lunaria is beyond your budget, a good alternative is to go for dessert. While enjoying the delicious French delicacies, you will be able to view the stage.

MAISON MAGNOLIA, Los Angeles
2903 South Hoover Street
(213) 746-1314
Dinner is $100 per person, including cocktail and wine;
brunch is $35 per person

Call for directions.

If you hadn't heard about this uncommon treasure of a restaurant you would have no idea it existed. The rather plain, blue-framed building is on a busy street near downtown Los Angeles. There are no telltale signs that this is anything other than someone's modest home. But once you get your reservations and show up for dinner or brunch, you discover the beautifully arranged dining room, living room, and small study. Maison Magnolia is a cross between a private dinner party and a four-star restaurant. There is room for only 20 guests, and most of the seating is shared. This somewhat compulsory socialization with people you don't know is a drawback, but you can request a table for two and focus on each other and the food to come.

Dinner starts with cocktails and a splendid array of hors d'oeuvres in the small garden terrace. You are then escorted to your table and the parade of courses begins. Be prepared for an exquisite array of dishes that are done to perfection and for a lengthy stay; dinner here is an experience to be savored.

MILLER'S ACORN RANCH, Chatsworth
23360 Lake Manor Drive
(818) 888-2099
Moderate

Call for directions.

As you drive through the curvy hills on Lake Manor Drive, it is easy to forget that you are in Chatsworth. Barren stretches of land with scattered houses and ranches make you wonder if a restaurant exists along the windy street. Miller's Acorn Ranch is easy to miss, but keep your eyes open, because it is enchanting—well worth a visit. Resembling a small farmhouse in the middle of vast wilderness, the atmosphere inside is comfortable, warm, and inviting. With no more than 20 tables placed in front of a roaring fireplace, this is one of the coziest spots in the valley. Windows trimmed with lace, antique ceiling lamps, and shelves holding aged relics surround the homey dining room. Outside patio seating is also available. The basically American menu includes seafood, ribs, steaks, and pasta dishes. The food isn't great, but it is quite good.

MONICA'S, Santa Monica
2640 Main Street
(310) 392-4956
Moderate to Expensive

On Main Street off Ocean Park Avenue, eight blocks south of Pico.

Monica's is housed in a stunning Victorian mansion, but it isn't always easy to blend a Southern California dining experience with

Victorian elegance. Although Monica's tries its best, the waitpeople in shorts and polo shirts seem out of place. The setting is undeniably charming. Beveled glass windows fill the parlor, living room, and front room with prismatic light. An outdoor cedar patio is available for sunny afternoon repasts. The food is good and the menu varied. This is casual dining all the way. Still, with the right frame of mind, an evening out at Monica's can become a night of courting and wooing. Why miss the opportunity?

NIZETICH'S RESTAURANT, San Pedro
1050 Nagoya Street, Berth 80
(213) 514-3878
Expensive

Take the Harbor Freeway (Interstate 110) heading south to San Pedro and exit at Harbor Boulevard. Turn right on Harbor Boulevard and follow the ports-of-call signs overhead. At Sixth Street turn east, then go south on Nagoya. The restaurant is in a tall white building on your left before you reach the wharf area.

Overlooking Los Angeles Harbor, with a soothing view of reflected city lights, Nizetich's has an outdoor dining area where couples can watch ships passing in the night. The indoor dining is nice but a little too slick to be as winsome as its outside counterpart. If you journey down to the southern beaches, this is an inviting place to tickle your fancy with lunch, dessert, or a toast to your upcoming time together.

NUCLEUS NUANCE, West Hollywood
7267 Melrose Avenue
(213) 939-9888, (213) 939-9023
Moderate

From the Hollywood Freeway, exit at Highland Avenue. Drive to Melrose Avenue and turn right. The restaurant is between Poinsettia and Altavista, three blocks west of La Brea.

This isn't just any intimate, dimly lit gourmet restaurant; this is a jazz club par excellence. The entertainment changes nightly and the music is always great. On any given night you might find the band playing '40s-style dance tunes, nostalgia, Latin smoothies, jazz, or simply sounds that lull your stress away. This brand of music is always moving. The phrase "They're playing our song" was probably first whispered at a place like this.

◆ **Romantic Note**: On weekends there are three shows nightly: 9:30 P.M., 11:00 P.M., and 12:30 A.M.; expect a cover charge and two-drink minimum per person per show Friday and Saturday, or per night Sunday through Thursday. Call for reservations.

THE ODYSSEY, Granada Hills
15600 Odyssey Drive
(818) 366-6444
Moderate

From the Hollywood Freeway go to Interstate 5 North, and then to Interstate 118 West. Exit from I-118 at Sepulveda, turn right, go to Rinaldi, and take a left. Follow Rinaldi to Blucher, the first right. Follow signs to The Odyssey's parking lot.

The Odyssey provides a romantic dining environment. A huge fireplace, ultra-plush sofas and chairs, a flowing fountain, and one of the most spectacular views of the valley I've ever seen are all part of the setting. You can dine at a dramatic table near the window or at a cozy, secluded pastel booth sitting side-by-side facing the view. Both tables and booths are surrounded by small antiques, etched mirrors, and flowers. After dinner, the bar is the perfect place for lingering over the all-encompassing view. On Friday and Saturday nights dancing (easy, not disco) above the city lights can be the perfect ending to a romantic evening.

There is one drawback to all of this: The Odyssey has a limited menu with only a few entrees to choose from (very similar to Castaways and The Reef, same owners). In spite of the atmosphere, it might be best to dine elsewhere and stop by The Odyssey for drinks before dinner or dessert afterwards.

THE OMELETTE PARLOR, Santa Monica
2732 Main Street
(310) 399-7892
Very Inexpensive

From Pico Boulevard, head due west till you come to Main Street, where you turn south. The restaurant is on the west side of the street.

I believe that breakfast is romantic. Maybe it's the coffee commercials I've been raised on, the ones that show a couple smiling at each other through the steam of a morning cup of java. So I've been programmed to associate ardent clinging, breakfast, and a cup of coffee. Whether or not you buy any of that, The Omelette Parlor is a congenial, easygoing, breakfast-specialty kind of place where you can linger over egg creations and, yes, hot fresh-brewed coffee. Before you venture out to the beach or store-browsing, this is the place to have your cup of coffee, breakfast, and dreamy-eyed mornings together.

◆ **Romantic Warning:** Weekends at The Omelette Parlor produce long lines, which means that if you don't have a patient appetite or a Sunday paper to share, don't bother to go.

PACIFIC DINING CAR, Los Angeles
1310 West Sixth Street
(213) 483-6000, (310) 453-4000
Moderate to Expensive

Near downtown Los Angeles, west of the Harbor Freeway, on Sixth Street between Witmer and Hartford.

It's 2 in the morning and you're still talking, sharing stories, giggling at the late hour and about how you both never run out of things to talk about. When there is a lull in the conversation you cuddle in a fond embrace of appreciation and love. Then, right in the middle of this affectionate interlude, you both get a craving for apple pie or a big juicy hamburger or even breakfast. At a moment like this, Denny's is hardly the answer, but the Pacific Dining Car restaurant is. This adorable restaurant looks like an old-fashioned dining car on a steam locomotive crossing the country in search of gold and fame. The food is basic but good, and the early-morning breakfasts are fabulous. Nothing less than a Los Angeles landmark, the Pacific Dining Car is late-night (early-morning) romance at its best.

PAPA LOUIE'S, Santa Monica
2911 Main Street
(310) 392-4664
Moderate

Call for directions.

Papa Louie's is the best-kept secret of the Santa Monica/Venice area. Unenlightened pedestrians could easily walk by, thinking it just another Italian eatery. The front dining room is OK, but if you request a table in the back, the maitre d' will take you to the Secret Garden. A brick path leads to this irresistible dining spot with a half-dozen well-spaced tables outside in a patio area complete with umbrellas, a fountain, and a view of a trickling waterfall in front of blossoming trees. Outside heaters provide warmth, while Italian love songs and soft lighting provide a truly romantic atmosphere. If the food were better, this could be one of my favorite secrets, but the food is just good. The garden is wonderful.

PIONEER BOULANGERIE, Santa Monica
2012 Main Street
(310) 399-7771
Very Inexpensive to Moderate

On Main Street between Bay Street and Bicknell Avenue, one block south of Pico.

The Pioneer Boulangerie is a potpourri of dining opportunities all housed in a maze-like building that stretches across one square city block. The weathered, dark wood exterior surrounded by a plethora of parked cars is more foreboding than inviting. Inside is a delicatessen cornucopia with four separate restaurants, a pastry shop, a wine cellar, a deli, a gift shop, a flower concession, and a giant on-display brick oven and kitchen where many of the baked goods are produced. You can choose to eat in the trellised outdoor cafe, the casual French country-style indoor cafeteria, the upstairs Basque dining room, or the elegant lounge and dining room at the back. Each is truly fetching, with its own individual style and personality. As you may have guessed, this is a well-known spot and can be crowded. However, it is still worth exploring for yourselves.

PRIMI, Los Angeles
10543 West Pico Boulevard
(213) 475-9335
Expensive

Two blocks east of Westwood Boulevard.

Primi is one stunning restaurant. The casual dining room includes a long black lacquered bar and views of the slick open kitchen. To the right lies the sultry, romantic garden area. What makes this room unique is that the plants and trees are placed behind illuminated glass, so the dim dining area remains lit solely by table candles. The garden tables can still view the kitchen through a large glass pane that separates the rooms. Dinner and lunch are served seven days a week. It is a delectable Italian experience.

RAGAZZI, Long Beach
4020 Olympic Plaza
(213) 438-3773
Moderate

Call for directions.

Ragazzi offers sumptuous regional Italian cuisine in an oceanfront bistro setting. Located next to the Long Beach pier, Ragazzi was designed to recreate the mood of coastal Italy. The authentic recipes were collected from Torino, Bozen, Bologna, Firenza, and Potenza, among others. Every seat offers a view. The outdoor dining is directly over the beach, with a huge fire pit and decorative lights. After dinner, a coastal stroll is only steps away.

THE REEF, Long Beach
880 Harbor Scenic Drive
(213) 435-8013
Expensive

Take the Long Beach Freeway (Highway 710) south, following the signs to Port of Queen Mary/Long Beach. Exit at Harbor Scenic Drive, turn left at the stop sign, and follow Harbor Scenic Drive underneath the overpass. Take a left at the second stop sign and The Reef will be on the corner.

There are not many restaurants in Los Angeles where you can dine in a French country setting, next to a glowing fireplace, with a spectacular view of the city lights reflecting off calm water. From the overstuffed sofas in the entrance to the downstairs cafe to the outdoor patio dining area directly overlooking the harbor, The Reef is large but nonetheless cozy. Each intimate booth is surrounded by bookshelves, lantern candles, and small antiques. For even more privacy, specify an upstairs booth toward the back of the room when making reservations. The small menu, which emphasizes California-style fish and pasta dishes, is only somewhat reliable, but the atmosphere is really the high point here.

REX-II RISTORANTE, Los Angeles
517 Olive Street
(213) 627-2300
Expensive to Very Expensive

On Olive Street, between Sixth and Seventh.

If you are staying near the downtown area and want to splurge on an evening of song, food, and dance, then take a short taxi ride over to Rex-II Ristorante. This highly acclaimed restaurant is exceptionally beautiful, with a rare 1940s flavor that is as dazzling as it is enchanting, and it is one of the few places in Los Angeles where you can dance slowly to live music and dine in choice style on excellent Italian cuisine. (On occasion, though, Rex's reputation is more impressive than its substance. During our last visit the carpet was badly stained and in need of replacement, and the entertainment in the lounge was not very entertaining. Still, the overall impression is beautiful and indeed elegant.)

RIVE GAUCHE, Palos Verdes
320 Tejon Place
(213) 378-0267
Moderate to Expensive

Call for directions.

Set in a quaint shopping area just off the main street in Palos Verdes, Rive Gauche is a traditional, extremely attractive place for dinner and leisurely romantic conversation. This is a popular local spot. Occasionally the quality of the food isn't top notch, but when it's good it's very, very good. Lunch is served every day but Monday, and dinner is served seven days a week.

SADDLE PEAK LODGE, Calabasas
419 Cold Canyon Road
(818) 222-3888
Expensive

Take Malibu Canyon Road north from Highway 1. Malibu Canyon Road turns into Las Virgenes Road. Just after you cross a bridge, turn right onto Piuma Road. Saddle Peak Lodge is at the intersection of Cold Canyon Road and Piuma Road.

If you have had enough of beach life and are ready for something completely different, head your wheels a short distance east from Malibu to Saddle Peak Lodge. You'll feel that you've traveled to another world. Whoever designed this rambling wood hideaway must have grown up mesmerized by *Bonanza*. The building itself, a huge sprawling log cabin that climbs up four stories along a rocky point in the middle of nowhere, has imposing stone fireplaces, rough-hewn oversize furniture, and interesting Western motifs wherever you turn. If the weather permits, you can sit outside on a stone patio that has a small trickling waterfall all its own. Here you can watch the valley succumb to nightfall as you sip a warm brandy or a hot cup of coffee. This is indeed an insular place for country dining, where you'll feel far removed from those you don't want to be near and nearer to the one you're with.

◆ **Romantic Note:** This remote location has no streetlights, so nighttime isn't only dark, it's really dark. Be careful and go slowly; you could pass by the lodge and never know you'd missed it.

TRYST, Los Angeles
401 North La Cienega Boulevard
(310) 289-1600
Expensive

On La Cienega, between Beverly and Melrose.

Sometimes you want a distinctive setting for a romantic liaison. Tryst lives up to its name. First, be aware that you could pass by this new restaurant without noticing it. From the street, it appears to be a dark, shades-drawn building; the hard-to-find entrance is on a narrow dead-end street, which after all is quite befitting the spirit of the place. Inside, ornate, one-of-a-kind light fixtures unobtrusively illuminate paneled walls hung with paintings of cherubs and cupids. The main dining room is replete with big comfy booths and tables with ample leather chairs. Large mirrors lined with jeweled lights surround the tables, giving the room a rose-colored glow. Once you've settled in, order a plate or two of Tryst's bite-size appetizers, designed so that you can finger-feed your dining companion provocative delicacies.

Outdoor Kissing

ANGELES NATIONAL FOREST
ANGELES CREST HIGHWAY TO CHARLTON FLATS

Take Interstate 210 north of Los Angeles to the Angeles Crest Highway.

The Angeles Crest Highway follows a dramatic path into the heart of the Angeles National Forest. As you follow its tendril-like course, each bend in the road exposes an abrupt change in the perspective and dynamics of the landscape. One curve may reveal a deep ravine framed by perilous mountain peaks, while another manifests a procession of massive golden hills weaving their way to eternity. Imagine the fervor you'll feel in the midst of these constant scenic transformations. The oohs and aahs that escape from deep in your throat will be echoed by the smiling person sitting next to you.

Did you remember to bring a basket of goodies? Mountain picnics have a flavor all their own; the combination of altitude (Charlton Flats is 5,300 feet straight up from sea level), fresh air, lofty pinery, and stupendous views whet the appetite and the heart. Charlton Flats offers all that, and privacy too. Even during the weekend, this area receives few visitors.

FRANKLIN MURPHY
SCULPTURE GARDENS, Westwood
University of California Los Angeles campus

Follow Sunset Boulevard to Hildegard, turn south, and enter the campus at the Wynton Street entrance. After you enter, take the first right and go straight for about three blocks. The gardens, which are next to the MacGowan Hall of Theatre Arts, will be on your left.

On Sunday, when the rest of the city and the college kids are everywhere but here, pack a picnic basket and bask in the privacy of this fascinating campus setting. Metal sculptures are displayed in symmetrical rows throughout grounds shaded by Japanese-style knotted trees and shrubbery. Places like this often trigger the imagination, so be sure to listen carefully as you wander here. Poetic words by Shakespeare, Keats, and Browning seem to whisper through the sturdy boughs, teasing lovers with their passionate messages. (If one-liners by Neil Simon interrupt the message, move your blanket.)

◆ **Romantic Suggestion:** After whiling away the morning at the gardens, couples too impatient to organize a picnic might consider having brunch at **HAMLET GARDEN RESTAURANT**, 1139 Glendon, Westwood, (213) 824-1818, (Moderate to Expensive), at the corner of Lindbrook and Glendon. This appealing restaurant, not even vaguely college-oriented, serves satisfying meals ranging from delicious casual snacks to full dinners.

GONDOLA EAST GETAWAYS, Long Beach
5437 East Ocean Boulevard
(310) 433-9595
$50 an hour for two people

Call for directions.

Gondola Getaways is a California version of old-world boating, right in the heart of Long Beach. Authentic Venetian gondolas cruise the narrow canals and waterways of Naples Island, next to the resort area of Belmont Shores. These narrow waterways (pollution-free, by the way), lined by architecturally unique homes and draped by brick foot-bridges, are remarkably secluded.

As you arrange yourself in your gondola, you are handed a warm blanket to snuggle under. A basket of bread, cheeses, and salami is provided so you can leisurely feed each other while drinking the beverage you bring (they provide glasses and an ice bucket). A gondolier gently guides the boat through the beautiful canals, accompanied by classical music. Nighttime cruises are especially romantic, as the moonlight spreads a golden reflection over the water.

◆ **Romantic Note:** Reservations are required, at least a week prior to date. Gondola Getaways is open seven days a week, from 11 A.M. to 11 P.M. Other boats are available that carry eight to 14 or 20 to 40 people.

HIGH TIMES, Moor Park
896 Warren Circle
(805) 522-8183
Very Expensive

Call for reservations and directions to the takeoff and landing sites.

Once in a lifetime you should treat yourselves to a frivolous, madcap encounter with the clouds and sky. The gondola of a hot-air balloon is one of the few vehicles built for two that provides just such an opportunity. A morning spent moving heavenward will surpass your wildest expectations.

Your excursion commences at sunrise. You step into the gondola, your pulse beginning to race with expectation. As the wind guides your craft up and over the countryside, the earth looks more peaceful than you thought possible. You may also be startled at the splendor of sunrise from this vantage point, as daylight awakens the hills with new vigor and color. When your flight is over, take time to discuss how being carried away has taken on a new meaning that the two of you will never forget.

◆   **Romantic Note:** Other balloon companies in the area include: **A BALLOON RIDE ADVENTURE,** (213) 451-4233; **GREAT AMERICAN BALLOON COMPANY,** (800) 272-3631; and **AIR AFFAIRE ENTERPRISES,** (800) 262-1979. The cost varies from $100 to $145 per person, and usually includes a champagne brunch.

THE HUNTINGTON LIBRARY
AND GROUNDS, San Marino
1151 Oxford Road
(818) 681-6601

Call for directions.

Libraries are not romantic unless you happen to be having an affair with a bookworm. On the other hand, 207 acres of magnificently sculpted gardens and woods are enticingly romantic. The landscape architects and horticultural geniuses who created this perennial wonderland fulfilled their deepest floral fantasies every inch of the way. The leas, glens, and forests are lavishly decorated with foliage and plant life. The cactus garden, rose garden, Zen garden, and Shakespearean garden are works of art that defy description. Ask someone special to accompany you hand-in-hand through these grounds: you'll surely find a corner of Eden you can call your own.

◆ **Romantic Note**: Avoid visiting the library on weekends unless the person you want to share this with is your Uncle Lou and his family. The library is closed on Mondays.

◆ **Romantic Suggestion**: There is an indoor-outdoor restaurant near the rose garden, or you can brave the city elements and have lunch or dinner at the **HOLLY STREET BAR AND GRILL**, 175 East Holly Street, Pasadena, (818) 440-1421, (Moderate). Housed in a quaint brick building, the restaurant's interior is disappointingly slick. However, the food is surprisingly good and the service cordial and attentive.

◆ **Second Romantic Suggestion:** **JULIENNE**, 2649 Mission Street, San Marino, (818) 441-2299, (Inexpensive), is a quaint little French cafe that is probably one of the finest in the area. The food is exquisite, the aromas heavenly, and the lovely interior features tile floors, windows shaded with lace, and wall mirrors draped in forest green. A cappuccino with a fresh baked muffin or bread or a slice of thick, creamy light quiche can be a lovely finale to a long day of exploring the gardens at the Huntington Library.

THE J. PAUL GETTY MUSEUM, Malibu
17985 Pacific Coast Highway
(310) 458-2003

Just off the Pacific Coast Highway, north of Santa Monica and south of Malibu.

From the moment you set foot upon these august grounds, it is apparent that the Getty is not just any museum. The palace-like building houses a superlative collection of drawings by the old masters, 19th-century paintings, antique manuscripts, and antique furnishings that once belonged to European nobility. The grounds are enhanced by pathways lined with ponds, sculpted gardens, and courtyards. As you pass through each corridor, over marble flooring that leads through ornate rooms showcasing the art collection, you will be drawn into the mood and richness of the setting. Perhaps this isn't what you would call a good place in which to kiss, but it surely is an inspirational prelude to just that sort of interaction.

OCEANFRONT WALK, Venice

Take Washington Boulevard east from Marina Del Rey to Pacific Avenue and turn south. Continue for 10 short blocks to Hurricane Street and park. The beaches are due west for the next two miles.

This isn't the part of Venice you're thinking of. Actually, it's hard to imagine that there is a beach anywhere in the Los Angeles area that isn't consumed by locals and tourists alike. I searched for a long time to find a stretch of unoccupied shoreline. Just as my options seemed to be dwindling, when I least expected it, there it was.

I was driving west along Washington Boulevard, planning to turn north along the coast, when I made a wrong turn south trying earnestly to avoid Venice Beach. The street I turned onto looked more like an alley than a street. The area was lined with small condominium-type apartment buildings. The units on the west side of the street all bordered an expansive beach that was everything a beach should be: spacious, white, uncluttered, secluded ... and vacant. Ah, the feeling of a gentle beach getaway: the softness of the sun enveloping you in a warm blush, a cushion of sand underneath your blanket, the surf's pulsating, rhythmic splashing onto the shore. Is it any wonder that the right beach with the right someone can provide the ultimate in romance? There are other sections of beach like this elsewhere, particularly down south and farther north, and if the temperature is below Southern California standards most of them will be empty. This location is kissing-reliable in almost any kind of weather.

POINT DUME BEACH, Malibu

Head north on the Pacific Coast Highway to Westward Beach Road. Turn left and follow the road to its end, at the parking lot below Point Dume. From the southern end of the parking lot, head out across the sand and look for the well-marked trail on the left.

Point Dume Beach is one of the most delightful beaches this area has to offer. The shore is surrounded by cascading golden palisades and dotted with overflowing tide pools; the surf is far less populated than at better-known and overcrowded Zuma Beach to the north. The only reason for the small numbers here is the remoteness of the area; access to this locale requires some degree of surefootedness and the desire to walk about a mile. Point Dume is not so remote that you will be the only ones lurking about, but your privacy needs should be fulfilled here. On a clear day from Point Dume you can see the entire rugged coastline making its way south to Catalina Island, which seems to float in the middle of a calm, measureless blue realm. Be patient enough to wait for sunset, when the sky will stage a stunning performance just for the two of you.

◆ **Romantic Note:** The evening air can become chilly at the beach, so bring a sweater or a cover-up if you plan to watch the sunset comfortably.

TOPANGA CANYON
Topanga State Park
20825 Entrada Road
(310) 455-2465

Take Interstate 10 west to the Pacific Coast Highway and turn left. Follow the Pacific Coast Highway to Route 27 (Topanga Canyon Boulevard) and head north. At Entrada Road turn left to the park entrance.

I think that statistical-type information is not the least bit romantic. It's great if you're a surveyor, but it's not a basis for snuggling or affection. For example, knowing that Topanga State Park is the second-largest urban park in the nation (9,000 acres), with terrain that ranges from 200 feet to 2,400 feet above sea level, won't necessarily do a thing for you. What might prove more enticing is knowing that you are likely to fall in love with acre after seemingly endless acre of chaparral-covered wildland colored by multihued winter grasses and adorned with perennial flora and foliage. Now that has meaning! You can almost feel the ground move beneath your quickening feet as you see the crest of a hill looming before you. As you stand at the top and the ocean reveals itself nestled between interwoven hills, the only sound you'll hear is that of your lungs regaining their composure. The hiking here is ideal and more than worth a day trip away from the city.

The number of spectacular canyon hikes in the mountains surrounding the Los Angeles area is too great to outline properly in this type of book. Realistically, not everyone who wants romance has a pair of hiking boots or, for that matter, thighs that can handle the job. For those who have, I strongly recommend two books by Dennis Gagnon: *Hike Los Angeles: Volume 1* and *Hike Los Angeles: Volume 2*. Then you can climb, walk, or saunter to your heart's content through the backwoods of LA. Be sure to read about the hikes through **COLD CREEK CANYON PRESERVE**. This area is a paradise of running creeks, plummeting waterfalls, and, depending on the season, one of the most spectacular arrays of flora and fauna to be seen anywhere.

WATTLES PARK, Hollywood

Take La Brea Avenue to Hollywood Boulevard, turn north, then turn west on Curson. The park is at the intersection of Curson and Franklin.

The Los Angeles area is blessed with dozens of parks. Unfortunately, most of them are inundated by things nature never intended to grow there: drug dealers, loud teenagers, muggers, plus multitudes of harmless locals who want to feel grass under their feet. There are also the occasional lovers strolling in and out of the debris (or rolling around in the debris, oblivious to the goings on about them). Is there no refuge for those who want to appreciate the outdoor life in a more composed setting? Yes, there is: a park named Wattles.

When you first encounter the fenced boundaries of the park, you'll wonder if you made a mistake in reading the directions, but don't worry—you really are here. Half of this park is a cooperative garden, with a hodgepodge of crops and plants (not exactly a place you want to go traipsing through). The other half of the park includes a cloistered array of palm trees, stone benches, and a thriving fish pond in need of repair. At the far end of the grounds is a stone-edged path that coils up an amber-colored hillside. The hilltop view opens onto the canyon below. Wattles Park is a green refuge where you are likely to find yourselves with no distractions except the sound of your own voices and laughter.

◆ **Romantic Note:** Another park option is the southern tip of **GRIFFITH PARK**, located at the corner of Los Feliz and Western Avenue, heading north on Fern Dell Drive into the park. Here wooden bridges ford flowing streams that cascade over rocks, and thick foliage shades you wherever you go. This special forest refuge may prove to be the secluded outdoor spot you were looking for.

WHALE WATCHING, Malibu

The locations for potential whale sightings are too numerous to list here. Depending on the area you're in, either call the Visitors Bureau or the Chamber of Commerce for specific information.

Most people nowadays hold whales in high esteem. Maybe it's because we're excited at knowing that such immense and powerful creatures can glide through the ocean with such playful agility and speed. Or because we cherish the chance of connecting with a great mammal that knows the secrets of the aquatic world that we humans can only briefly visit and elusively understand. Whatever the reason, the search for whales is one you need to share with someone. Together you can come to witness what to anyone's way of thinking is surely a miracle.

◆ **Romantic Note:** Whale watching begins in late December and continues through late March. Point Dume Beach is a great place to seek out whales and to spend time alone outdoors.

◆ **Romantic Suggestion:** If you want to closer to the action, contact **WHALE WATCH,** in Redondo Beach at the Sport Fishing Pier, (310) 372-3566. Their boat may be crowded, but the close-up thrill you'll get exceeds that of offshore viewing.

WILL ROGERS
STATE HISTORIC PARK, Pacific Palisades
14253 West Sunset Boulevard
(213) 454-8212

Follow Sunset Boulevard west to the park.

For those in need of hiking territory close to Los Angeles, this eucalyptus-lined estate is stirring, and the surrounding hills that shape the backyard's acreage are glorious. The chaparral-covered slopes, pale green and gold, have paths that wind up and around to breathtaking vistas of the ocean to the west and the city to the south and east. The museum celebrating Will Rogers' life is interesting, but it won't ignite impetuous conversation or interaction. The polo grounds here host exciting weekend matches, but watching grown men maneuver sweaty stallions around a field as they chase a small ball with a mallet is not everyone's idea of affection-inspiring activity. (In spite of that discouraging description, you should witness this sport at least once, just to see what it's like.)

"Kissing is a means of getting two people so close together that they can't see anything wrong with each other."

Rene Yasenek

"*I tried to resist his overtures but he plied me with symphonies, quartets, chamber music, and cantatas.*

S.J. Perelman

ORANGE COUNTY

Anaheim and Brea

Restaurant Kissing

THE CELLAR, Anaheim　　　　　　　　　　　◆◆◆
305 North Harbor Boulevard
(714) 525-5682
Expensive

Call for directions.

The artistic crew from Disneyland designed The Cellar restaurant in 1969. What makes dining here so engaging is that the three main dining rooms are located underground. Private, secluded, exclusive booths are placed around a room filled with roaring open fireplaces, magnificent statues, and crystal chandeliers. The cavernous stone walls are decorated with silver lanterns, antiques, artwork, and wine casks. Eating at The Cellar is like being in the French wine country, enjoying classic French/European cuisine, with a bit of Disney fantasy sprinkled on top.

Be sure to ask your waiter for a tour of the upstairs cellars where the wine is stored. The restaurant carries more than 800 different wines, ranging in price from $50 to $1,500.

◆　**Romantic Suggestion:** The Cellar holds afternoon wine tasting sessions that take place in the wine cellars. There you can sample rare wines from France, champagnes, and imports from Europe, Canada, and Australia, while learning a great deal about the history of wine making.

JW'S, Anaheim
Anaheim Marriott Hotel
700 West Convention Way
(714) 750-8000
Expensive

Take Interstate 5 South to Harbor Boulevard and turn right. Follow Harbor to the third traffic signal and turn right onto Convention Way. The hotel is two blocks south of Disneyland.

Step into JW's and you will be immediately transported to an English country house with high ceilings and 19th-century details. Hardwood floors and brick walls add to the classic atmosphere. Every room is different, with original artwork, fireplaces, candelabras, glass paneling, fabric wall coverings, and handsome antique furnishings. A harpist plays from 6:30 P.M. to 10:30 P.M. The traditional French menu is creative and brilliantly prepared. JW's fully deserves its *Orange Coast* magazine title as the "Best Table in Orange County."

LA VIE EN ROSE, Brea
240 South State College Boulevard
(714) 529-8333
Expensive to Very Expensive

On State College Boulevard off Imperial Highway, across the street from the Brea Mall.

This stunning restaurant, designed to be a replica of a Normandie farmhouse, succeeds in every regard. The octagonal steepled ceiling, the tapestry-covered walls, the small intimate dining rooms with handsome appointments are part of the effect. A spiral staircase leads upstairs to an intimate alcove with a handful of tables. In the mansion's lounge, warmed by a glowing fireplace, a mandolin and pianist serenade throughout the evening. The Provencal menu reads like a dream. Try the sea bass in a perfect cilantro coulis or the pate of veal and shrimp. It isn't easy to get to Brea, but La Vie en Rose is worth the trip.

MR. STOX, Anaheim
1105 East Katella Avenue
(714) 634-2994
Expensive

One block west of State College Boulevard on East Katella.

Large restaurants are rarely romantic. Crowds of people, even well spaced, are just not the hallmark of an intimate setting. Despite that, Mr. Stox is one of the more romantic restaurants I've seen. Seating over 260 people, it still manages to be an award-winning restaurant, both for kissing and cuisine. Although the black leather booths are oversized, you can sit as close to your dining partner as you desire.

There is a choice of dining rooms here, each with its own atmosphere. In one room you can be seated at a cozy table surrounded by Renaissance artwork, Persian carpets, and beautiful flowers. Another dining room affords a view of the wine cellar through a brick-framed window. Here the floor is cobblestone, the fireplace huge, and the decor resembles a European chateau. After dinner, the lounge features cheek-to-cheek dancing to live piano music. This beautiful setting is illuminated by a roaring fire and candlelit wall lamps.

Mr. Stox grows all its own herbs and makes all its pastas and pastries in-house.

THEE WHITE HOUSE, Anaheim
887 South Anaheim Boulevard
(714) 772-1381
Expensive

On Anaheim Boulevard between Ball and Lincoln.

This colonial-style Craftsman home was built in 1909. When it became a restaurant in 1981, the owner's sister worked out the political motif and fashioned the exterior after *The* White House. The interior of the home has been restored in an elegant, charming, understated manner, with most rooms retaining their original shape and size. Each of the three main downstairs dining rooms and five smaller upstairs rooms are different, and most contain no more than five tables. Gaze into your partner's eyes while sharing a delicious northern Italian meal in front of a warm fireplace, surrounded by lace curtains, pastel flowered walls, and beautiful antiques. The atmosphere and the food are excellent.

Newport Beach

Hotel/Bed and Breakfast Kissing

DORYMAN'S INN, Newport Beach
2102 West Ocean Front
(714) 675-7300, (800) 634-3303
Moderate to Unbelievably Expensive

Take the Pacific Coast Highway south and turn west onto Newport Boulevard, then west on Balboa Boulevard. A few blocks down, turn west onto MacFadden Place and proceed straight to Ocean Front Street, just in front of the Newport Pier.

The Doryman is so enticing that you will want to embrace immediately after you enter the front door. Everything about this bed and breakfast suggests silky Victorian affluence. The renovation is strikingly modern but so handsomely done that nothing in the place looks less than 100 years old. The floral green-trellised wallpaper flows gently through comfy rooms with marble bathrooms and Jacuzzi tubs, ocean views, sumptuous breakfasts, afternoon tea, and spacious boudoirs with sitting rooms. The sumptuous breakfasts and afternoon teas are delightful. If there's a slight chill in the air and the fog is drifting in from the ocean, follow a brisk morning walk on the pier with breakfast served in your sturdy four-poster canopied bed. The fire will crackle warmly on the hearth as you open your balcony doors to let in the day.

FOUR SEASONS HOTEL, Newport Beach
690 Newport Center Drive
(714) 759-0808, (800) 332-3442
Very Expensive to Unbelievably Expensive

From Pacific Coast Highway, take Newport Center Road north.

Located across from Fashion Island, this resort is elegant from start to finish, the kind of place where your every need is anticipated and fulfilled. The rooms are really more like suites, each with a separate living room to lounge and snuggle in. The higher floors are the most sought-after; they offer panoramic views of the coast and Newport skyline. Guests can also enjoy a lap pool, Jacuzzi, tennis courts, and three restaurants. The only bad thing about staying at the Four Seasons is the sorrow of knowing you'll eventually have to return to the real world.

PORTOFINO BEACH HOTEL, Newport Beach
2306 West Ocean Front
(714) 673-7030
Moderate to Very Expensive

From Pacific Coast Highway turn west on Newport Boulevard, then right on 22nd Street, and right on Ocean Front Street to the end of Newport Pier's parking area.

Around the corner from Doryman's Inn is a simpler, brighter, more pastel renovation called Portofino. If the Doryman is booked, or you just want to spend less money, try this effervescent place. The 15 rooms have demure pink-and-peach interiors with views you can drink in from your Jacuzzi, private sun deck, or parlor area. Be sure to ask about their special package rates with some of the local restaurants.

Portofino's only drawback is its proximity to the parking lot for Newport Pier, which is often bustling with wayward surfers and enthusiastic crowds. For some tastes that may be an asset and not a liability.

◆ **Romantic Suggestion:** Portofino has added a dazzling restaurant right next door. **RENATO**, 2304 West Ocean Front, Newport Beach,

(714) 673-8058, (Inexpensive to Expensive), has an elegant Tuscan ambience and dishes up classic Italian fare and exhilarating ocean views.

Restaurant Kissing

GEORGE'S CAMELOT, Newport Beach
Lido Marine Village
3420 Via Oporto
(714) 673-3233
Moderate to Expensive

Within walking distance of Doryman's Inn. Walk or drive up Newport Boulevard to 32nd Street and, if you're driving, park; cars are not allowed on the Lido itself. Then walk left onto Via Oporto and through the gray building to the balcony walkway to Camelot.

This restaurant may not evoke the legendary Camelot, but it isn't exactly Burbank either. Instead, it is a sentimental, petite cafe draped in shades of forest green, with a ringside view of the harbor. Camelot is part of a row of shops that line a long wooden boardwalk. An afternoon lunch here will allow you time to watch sunbeams dancing on the water while a parade of boats proceed to and from the dock.

LE BIARRITZ, Newport Beach
414 North Old Newport Boulevard
(714) 645-6700
Expensive

Take Highway 55 to Newport Boulevard. One block before you reach the Pacific Coast Highway, turn left onto Hospital. Le Biarritz is on the corner of Hospital and North Old Newport Boulevard.

If you can't indulge your wanderlust by going to France, dinner at Le Biarritz can be a one-night alternative. Standing out from its Newport neighbors, Le Biarritz looks like a French chateau complete with ivy-mantled tower and brick facade. The rooms, filled with warmth and intimacy, are all different. My favorite was the Garden Room, with its brick walls, floral decor, lace curtains, and copper planters filled with cascading plants. The tables are well spaced and the feeling is cozy. The chef's creations rival any you would find in Europe, and the desserts— *ce sont magnifique.*

PASQUEL, Newport Beach
1000 Bristol Street
(714) 752-0107
Moderate

At the corner of Bristol and Jamboree.

Along the Pacific Coast there are those who would suggest that a proper romantic evening has to come with an ocean view. Although a view is nice, there is something to be said about sharing an intimate table in a cozy place with good food, good wine, and waiters who are savvy enough to be there when you need them and scarce when you don't. A place like Pasquel.

Located in a small shopping area, Pasquel is a refreshing surprise from the moment you enter the door. Large bouquets of fresh flowers are everywhere you look, and an immense floral mural has been painted onto its white brick wall. The decor is country French and so is the food. The owner/chef, Pasquel, and his wife came here from France, bringing all their carefully guarded secrets for culinary excellence. The aroma of garlic perfumes the air here, and warm feelings abound. It's not unusual to find Pasquel leaving the kitchen to introduce himself and make sure you are happy with your meal. While you've got him, you may want to let him know that you are pleased not only with his fine cuisine (which I'm sure you will be), but with the romantic bit of France he has transported to Newport Beach.

THE RITZ, Newport Beach
880 Newport Center Drive
(714) 720-1800
Moderate to Expensive

From Pacific Coast Highway, head east on Newport Center Drive.

Elegant, opulent, and yes, even a bit gaudy, is how I'd describe this lavish continental restaurant. However, the glitz is what has made The Ritz such a popular spot for romantic dining. People love to come here on special occasions, dressed to the hilt. Bejeweled and bedecked in their finest attire, they eat rich food, sip expensive wine, and enjoy the restaurant's show-stopping presentations.

On one side of the restaurant, dark woods and deep burgundy leather inspire a classically romantic atmosphere; in another room peach walls, ornate mirrors, and gilded frames create a lighter, more baroque ambience. Dishes such as spit-roasted rack of lamb and bouillabaisse with lobster have made this an awarding-winning restaurant, with attractions for food and romance connoisseurs alike.

21 OCEANFRONT, Newport Beach
2100 West Ocean Front
(714) 675-2566
Moderate to Expensive

Take Balboa Boulevard south and turn west on McFadden Place. Follow it around the corner to West Ocean Front, just in front of the Newport Pier.

As the sun plays out its final performance of the day, melting into the turquoise sea, 21 Oceanfront prepares for its nightly encore. Time and again, couples in search of romance come to this warm and elegant restaurant, expecting brilliant sunsets, attentive service, and fine cuisine. They never leave disappointed. Just a few hundred yards from the crashing waves, seafood and pasta are served in a graceful green-marble/black-accented interior reminiscent of the gaslight era. You may even want to pack a bag for the night: with the exquisite Doryman's Inn right upstairs, you can have everything your hearts need without traveling anywhere else.

THE VIEW LOUNGE AT
THE MARRIOTT HOTEL, Newport Beach
900 Newport Center Drive
(714) 640-4000
Moderate

From Interstate 405, take Jamboree west. Turn left onto Santa Barbara. The Marriott will be on your right.

Chain hotels like the Marriott or the Sheraton rarely, if ever, meet the romantic standards of this kissing travel series. It's not that these places can't be extravagant and luxurious; it's just that they are often cavernous, loud, and business-oriented, qualities that don't promote affection and cuddling. The View Lounge is an exception.

Picture a sea of shimmering lights and sunset colors that gently fade into a cobalt night dotted by stars and a vibrant moon. That's what awaits you every evening: stretching from Long Beach to Laguna Beach, the spellbinding view from this lounge may be the best in all of Orange County. Listen to one of the many bands playing here nightly, or drop by on a Sunday night when the stage is empty and so is the lounge. There's nothing like having a brilliant sunset all to yourselves.

Outdoor Kissing

INSPIRATION POINT, Newport Beach
3100 block of Breakers Drive

From East Pacific Coast Highway, take Marigold south to Breakers Drive.

Yes, there really is an Inspiration Point and you can bet it's been the inspiration for many a romantic encounter over the years. Too small to be called a park, but more lush than your average lookout, this is a great place to bring a picnic basket and someone you love. With any luck, you'll find the tiny mound of grass overlooking the sparkling sea reserved just for you, but if not, you can enjoy the surrounding splendor from the nearby benches or on the terrace just down the hill.

Inspiration Point is the kind of place where people come to write poetry, propose marriage, or even exchange "I do's." Flowers encircle the bluff and grow in colorful patches all the way down the cliffs. Though there isn't a home around here that costs less than a million dollars, wealth comes in many forms. Sharing nature's resplendence with someone you love is worth more than its weight in gold.

◆ **Romantic Alternatives:** Other local spots of inspiration include **KING'S ROAD PARK**, Kings Road at St. Andrews Road, a pictur-esque pocket park overlooking the shore, and **GALAXY PARK**, Galaxy Drive at Mariners Drive, which provides a beautiful vista of the lagoon and the Newport skyline. The only sounds you're likely to hear around here will be the birds singing in the trees and the gardeners snipping the bushes of the perfectly manicured estates that surround it.

IRVINE COAST CHARTERS, Newport Beach
Lido Marina Village
3416 Via Oporto, Suite 204
(714) 675-4704
Unbelievably Expensive and Beyond

Call for directions.

If you are anxious to let your love set sail, these are the people to talk to. How about a yacht cruise, complete with staff to serve you a candlelight gourmet meal? Better yet, why not a romantic gondola ride around the bay, followed by a vessel filled with string musicians to serenade you? Dream it up and this company will make your *Love Boat* fantasies come true.

Balboa

Hotel/Bed and Breakfast Kissing

BALBOA INN, Balboa
105 Main Street
(714) 675-3412
Moderate to Expensive

Newport Boulevard heading south from Newport Pier becomes Balboa Street. Take Balboa to Main Street and you're there.

This picturesque Spanish-style inn, a stone's throw from the Balboa Pier, is an out-of-the-way, right-in-the-middle-of-things combination of hotel and bed and breakfast. The rooms, as eclectic as their prices, all have different influences and personalities. No matter what price range you can afford, all the rooms have a seaside-resort atmosphere. The ocean is so close you can see the waves roll onto the sand, hear the surf lash against the shore, smell the ocean breeze, and taste the salt in the air.

Balboa is abandoned by tourists in the off-season, which opens it up for the lovers of the world to enjoy. In comparison to Laguna or Newport, this is a sequestered location where the beach is sublime, the sunsets provocative, and the air sweet and pure.

◆ **Romantic Suggestion:** Whale-watching charters are available at the Balboa Pavilion, two blocks away from the Balboa Inn. Get directions from the front desk or concierge.

Restaurant Kissing

BRITTA'S CAFE, Balboa
205 Main Street
(714) 675-8146
Inexpensive to Moderate

Take Balboa Boulevard to Main Street and turn left.

Problem: After an arduous day of sightseeing, you're ready for a quiet, romantic dinner but you just don't have it in you to get all dressed up. Answer: Try Britta's, one of the few places I've found where candlelight, shorts, and sandals seem to go together. Just down the street from the Newport Pier and around the corner from the playful Fun Zone, this charming little cafe is popular with the suntanned locals.

Here the coffee smells of cinnamon and fresh flowers adorn every table. Though not fancy by any means, Britta's has a sort of underlying refinement. Maybe it's the walls lined with the work of local artists, or perhaps it's the soft classical music that fills the room. It could be the unexpected quality of its food; Britta's is attached to a gourmet kitchen shop and you can quickly tell a pro is at work. The food is simple but lovingly prepared; pasta, meat dishes, and sandwiches make up the bulk of the menu. Don't stop there, though—the dessert tray is calling your names.

TETE-A-TETE, Balboa Island
217 Marine Avenue
(714) 673-0570
Moderate

Take Jamboree Road west across the bridge to Balboa Island, where it turns into Marine Avenue.

There are small romantic restaurants. And then there are really small romantic restaurants. Tete-a-Tete is an intriguing example of the latter. Squeezed in between shops on the main drag of Balboa Island, the outside alone is enough to provoke your interest: it is reminiscent of a quaint country cabin, its flower box overflows with colorful blossoms, and reflections from the candlelight inside dance on the beveled edges of the cut-glass windows.

Inside, you may feel a tiny bit claustrophobic. Don't worry, though. Like a miner in a small cavern, you will quickly feel the thrill of knowing you've uncovered a precious jewel. Floral tapestry banquettes line both sides of the room, divided by an aisle. A handful of small tables, blushing in pink linens, occupy the space, making it intimate, though not very private. Still, the French-inspired food, the candlelight, and the romantic music create the kind of ambience made for whispering sweet nothings.

◆ **Romantic Alternative**: Just up the street you'll find **AMELIA'S**, 311 Marine Avenue, Balboa Island, (714) 673-6580, (Inexpensive to Moderate). This Italian restaurant has been here for more than 30 years, as the mementos covering its walls illustrate. Though these nostalgic touches don't really add to the romance, they don't hinder it either. A corner table, some mouth-watering pasta, and a little Pavarotti playing in the background will surely result in a most memorable evening.

Outdoor Kissing

BALBOA PAVILION AND FUN ZONE, Balboa

Take Balboa Boulevard to Main Street and turn left.

The Balboa Fun Zone is perfectly delightful entertainment for any-one who's tired of being an adult. Turn off the fax machine, put down the cellular phone, and walk down the boardwalk that is Newport's answer to Coney Island. Eat cotton candy to your heart's delight, take silly pictures in the photo booths, play "keep away" in the bumper cars, and ride the colorful carousel. After dark, a spin on the ferris wheel will not only provide you with a spectacular view of the lights along the water, but a marvelous spot to sneak a few kisses.

◆   **Romantic Suggestion:** During the day, sightseeing cruises leave the harbor about every half hour. The **PAVILION QUEEN, (714) 673-5245)**, a pretty double-deck Mississippi-style paddleboat, will float you past the expensive yachts, million-dollar homes, and winding channels that make Newport legendary.

BALBOA ISLAND

Take Jamboree straight to Marine Street or board the ferry at the Fun Zone in Balboa.

If you'd like to find something fun and romantic to do in Newport Beach, consider taking the ferry to Balboa Island. Leaving from the Balboa Fun Zone, the three-car ferry has been around since the 1920s and transports passengers, animals, and bicycles as well. As you cross the small channel, you can't help but gape at the incredible estates that line the island. Just between you and me, Balboa Island isn't really an island though it might as well be. It is Fantasy Island-clean, beautiful and outrageously expensive. The houses seem like an endless potpourri of gingerbread confections, some Cape Cod-style, others right out of a Hans Christian Andersen storybook. On Marine Street, you'll find an enticing assortment of restaurants and specialty shops to wander through hand-in-hand. Or slip away to the water's edge to enjoy a picnic and perhaps a kiss or two.

Corona Del Mar

Restaurant Kissing

FIVE CROWNS RESTAURANT, Corona Del Mar
3801 East Pacific Coast Highway
(714) 760-0331
Moderate to Expensive

At the corner of East Pacific Coast Highway and Poppy.

Although Five Crowns is rather large, with many tables scattered throughout, the atmosphere is endearing. Most couples have found a way to make the place their own, adopting a special table, a quiet corner, a favorite room. By one of the hearths or at a window table, they sip, they laugh, and they share loving conversation as though they were the only two people in the place. The traditional Cantonese cuisine is quite good and sometimes excellent.

◆ **Romantic Alternative:** Not far away is one of the area's most unusual restaurants, **TREES**, 440 Heliotrope, Corona Del Mar, (714) 673-0910, (Moderate). Once a private home, Trees gives you the feeling that you are dining in the house of a good friend, one with very abstract artistic taste. The dining rooms are stark, with walls clashing in color, and candlelight creating a dance of light and shadow. Some rooms are embellished by murals of trees or by real trees and twigs wrapped in tiny white lights. The food, as eclectic and abstract as the rest of the house, has won many awards.

ROTHSCHILD, Corona Del Mar
2407 East Pacific Coast Highway
(714) 673-3750
Moderate

At the intersection of MacArthur and East Pacific Coast Highway.

The job of looking for kissing places is a dream assignment for almost any travel writer. One occupational hazard of this job is that after exploring so many restaurants, both charming and not-so-charming, they all begin to look alike. How refreshing to find Rothschild!

This is the stuff adoring encounters are made of: an eclectic mix of fantasy and reality, old-world charm and Newport chic. Not only will you feast on some of the best northern Italian cuisine around, but your eyes can feast on handsome European antiques and 19th-century paintings. And as you share all of this with the one you love, you may just want to top off your evening with a kiss—a chocolate kiss that is a house specialty, made with the finest Belgian chocolate and laced with plump, juicy raspberries. It's almost as sweet as your anticipation of the night ahead.

Laguna Beach

Hotel/Bed and Breakfast Kissing

THE CARRIAGE HOUSE, Laguna Beach
1322 Catalina Street
(714) 494-8945
Moderate to Expensive

After you enter the business area of Laguna Beach, look for Cress Street and turn east. Go one block to Catalina; the house is at the intersection of Cress and Catalina.

Bed and breakfasts all have their own charming idiosyncrasies. Given the right touches, nothing is quite as affection-producing as staying in a home that has diligently considered the longings of the heart. These include the aroma of fresh-baked pastries first thing in the morning, downy quilts, antique bibelots and finery, and, of course, your own personal bathroom. The Carriage House is a perfect old-fashioned New Orleans-style bed and breakfast that turns just another weekend out of town into a lasting memory.

All the rooms here encircle a brick courtyard filled with tropical plants and flowers. Each of the six multihued rooms reflects a different part of the world, ranging from the English countryside to the Orient. You won't find a lot of ocean views from The Carriage House, simply a lot of comfort, privacy, and pleasure.

CASA LAGUNA INN, Laguna Beach
2510 South Pacific Coast Highway
(714) 494-2996, (800) 233-0449
Inexpensive to Very Expensive

The inn is two miles south of the main beach on the South Pacific Coast Highway.

Built in the 1930s, Casa Laguna's main house and cottages are a combination of California Mission and Spanish Revival styles. The *casitas* (little cottages), comprising 19 courtyard or balcony suites, were added in the '40s as word of Laguna's artist colony began to spread. The inn is settled into a hillside lush with lofty palm trees and tropical plants and flowers. The grounds also contain winding paths, an aviary, and a small greenhouse. There are several tiled terrace areas to lounge in, but sunsets are best enjoyed from the inn's intriguing bell tower or from the deck above the sparkling pool. It's pretty rare to find a bed and breakfast with a pool, much less one that overlooks the ocean. But then again, Casa Laguna Inn is not your average bed and breakfast.

The rooms are small but endearing, all with private bathrooms and antique furnishings. You can choose from a courtyard or ocean-view room, but you really should splurge on the cottage. Here you'll find everything you could want or need for an unforgettable night of romance. Besides enjoying the best view in the inn from its private deck, it also has a fireplace, a dear living room area, and a fully equipped kitchen for nights when you'd prefer to eat in. Of course, breakfast and afternoon tea are on the house.

◆ **Romantic Warning:** The only reason this charming inn doesn't get a higher rating is because of the constant hum of traffic from the

Pacific Coast Highway below. Chances are, though, the only sounds you'll hear will be the patter of your hearts.

EILER'S INN, Laguna Beach
741 South Pacific Coast Highway
(714) 494-3004
Moderate to Expensive

In Laguna Beach, right on the South Pacific Coast Highway. Watch for the numbers on buildings to judge your proximity to the inn.

During my research, I was concerned that any oceanside town near Los Angeles would be overrun with people who, just like me, were in search of a close-by, sequestered getaway. And it's true, the oceanside towns are stuffed to the gills with seclusion seekers, so one must do some pretty creative seeking to get away from the throngs. Eiler's Inn indeed feels removed from the masses, even though it is in the center of Laguna.

The picture-perfect, homey, guest house is constructed around a slightly disheveled brick New Orleans-style courtyard overgrown with thick plants and scattered with white wrought-iron tables and chairs. The relaxed atmosphere is accentuated by the bottle of champagne that greets you upon checking in and the hearty breakfast served fresh every morning. With the Pacific Ocean's turbulent surf beckoning at your back door, everything is in order for sparkling private time together.

HOTEL LAGUNA, Laguna Beach
425 South Pacific Coast Highway
(714) 494-1131, (800) 524-2927 in California
Inexpensive to Expensive

Right next to the main beach, on the South Pacific Coast Highway.

The best thing about this landmark hotel is its location in the very heart of Laguna Beach, just steps away from the ocean, the shops, and the tantalizing restaurants. Everything is right here. Once the haunt of Hollywood's biggest stars, Hotel Laguna was the first inn built in this area, more than 100 years ago. The present structure was erected in the

1930s and affectionately dubbed the "Grand Lady" by local historians.

Unfortunately, the "Grand Lady" is in need of a slight face-lift. Some of her hallways smell of mildew and most of the rooms are small and nondescript. However, the hotel's beautiful rose garden (popular for weddings) and ocean-view restaurants seem to make up for it somehow. The constant flow of bridal parties—mostly on weekends—adds a bit of romance and wonder to the place, while an afternoon tryst at **THE TERRACE** (not to be mistaken with The Terrace restaurant across the street) allows you to dine on mouth-watering Mexican food in the midst of sunshine and sea breezes. **CLAES'**, the handsome formal dining room, offers award-winning continental cuisine and what could be Laguna's most spectacular ocean view. Bathed in pink and brightened by bursts of fresh flowers, Claes' is the quintessential amorous place to dine.

INN AT LAGUNA BEACH, Laguna Beach
211 North Pacific Coast Highway
(714) 497-9722, (800) 544-4479
Moderate to Unbelievably Expensive

North of the main beach on the North Pacific Coast Highway.

Just on the other side of the main beach from Hotel Laguna is a newer, more modern alternative. The Inn at Laguna Beach may not have the grandeur of the larger hotel, but its rooms are much prettier and feature ocean-view terraces. Most are cloaked in the colors of the sea with walls embellished by the work of local artists. The amenities here include TV/VCRs, clock radios, robes, and microwave ovens. A rooftop sun deck and a beachside pool and spa await you as well. Better yet, follow the path from the lobby just a few steps to the water's edge. Romance has never been this convenient.

SURF AND SAND HOTEL, Laguna Beach
1555 South Pacific Coast Highway
(714) 497-4477, (800)524-8621
Moderate to Unbelievably Expensive

About one mile south of the main beach area on the South Pacific Coast Highway.

Occasionally, travel writers uncover a find so exciting that even the most flowery superlatives don't seem superlative enough. The Surf and Sand Hotel is such a find: everything about it is exquisite. Chalk it up to the hotel's recent $26 million renovation and its ideal location near the heart of Laguna Beach. From the moment the valet takes your car, you are transported into a world where your every need is lovingly looked after, and romance and relaxation seem to go hand in hand. All of the 156 rooms have ocean views and come-hither balconies that summon you to gaze at the glistening surf below. The color scheme is subdued and elegant, a mixture of bleached woods and creamy shades of beige. Plush robes, marble baths, and glass-enclosed showers make lounging here extra luxurious.

The hotel offers 500 yards of spectacular private beach, plus a seaside swimming pool. Two world-class restaurants are at your beck and call, as elegant and romantic as you could possibly hope for. **SPLASHES** is the more informal of the two, a light and airy restaurant enhanced by a flickering hearth, wall-to-wall ocean views, and the blending of classical music and the crashing waves below. **SPLASHES BAR**, just a few steps away, enjoys the same decor and splendid vistas.

THE TOWERS RESTAURANT is dramatically located nine stories above the surging sea. By day, the sparkling blue waters are reflected in the dining room's mirrored walls and ceiling. At sunset the room is alive with color, the crash of the waves below, and the hushed tones of spellbound lovers. The restaurant's muted green decor, chrome-and-glass art deco detailing, and flickering candlelight create an attractive setting for its inspired French cuisine. **THE TOWERS BAR** is an equally inviting place to toast the sunset. Enjoy an intimate conversation by the glow of the hearth, as soothing sounds emanate from the glass-topped piano bar.

The Surf and Sand deserves not only our highest rating of four kisses, but a few hugs to boot.

Restaurant Kissing

CEDAR CREEK INN, Laguna Beach
384 Forest Avenue
(714) 497-8696
Inexpensive to Moderate

On the corner of Forest Avenue and Third Street.

From the outside, Cedar Creek Inn looks like an enchanting English country home, complete with burgeoning flowers, wood-shingle roof, and colorful stained glass windows. The stately dining area is softened by floral curtains and oversize bouquets. The enormous stone hearth beckons lovers to find a table nearby, while the baby grand piano serenades them with soft, romantic melodies. The menu is quite varied, with items ranging from steak to seafood to sandwiches.

◆ **Romantic Suggestion:** Down the block you'll find **THE RE-NAISSANCE CAFE**, 234 Forest Avenue, Laguna Beach, (714) 497-JAVA, (Inexpensive to Moderate). This is a dynamic, ultramodern cafe, where locals like to sit on the front terrace and watch the world (and day) go by. Cloaked in black detailing and slick surfaces—with waiters dressed to match—the The Renaissance serves provocative California cuisine but is most popular for coffee, desserts, and lingering.

THE COTTAGE, Laguna Beach
308 North Pacific Coast Highway
(714) 494-8980
Inexpensive to Moderate

On the northeast corner of North Pacific Coast Highway and Aster Street.

The Cottage Restaurant is right out of a William Buffet painting: a 1910 beach bungalow filled with pastel-clad lovers enjoying breakfast served with a sea breeze and a crackling fireplace. On any weekend, you'll find locals and tourists alike waiting their turn to do brunch here. And why not? The food is hearty and inexpensive, the inside is comfortable and cozy, and the hint of an ocean view from the delightful garden patio is enough to melt the butter on your toast. The Cottage also serves lunch and dinner, but there's something about breakfast here that makes it the most romantic meal of the day.

FIVE FEET, Laguna Beach   💋
328 Glenneyre Street
(714) 497-4955
Moderate

One block south of Forest Avenue on Glenneyre.

If "nouveau romantic dining" isn't yet a term, it's time someone coined it. We need a phrase for the romantic spot that doesn't abide by the usual standards. A place like Five Feet.

This is a restaurant far ahead of its time (surely more than five feet). Centered around an open kitchen, the interior is futuristic, combining gray, black, and pink against a backdrop of concrete walls, neon lights, tubular steel chairs, and exotic flora. Abstract art lines the walls. The food itself is just as forward thinking. While some would consider it Chinese or Pacific Rim, I would call it, well, daring. After all, it's not every day you find goat cheese wontons with raspberry sauce, followed by an entree of Alaskan salmon grilled and dressed with a wild strawberry-basil relish. The menu changes every six weeks, so your choices may be a bit different. They will certainly be as eclectic.

◆ **Romantic Alternative:** Let's say Five Feet doesn't quite measure up to your romantic standards. How about a more mainstream alternative? Just a few doors down, **THE SORRENTO GRILLE**, 370 Glenneyre, Laguna Beach, (714) 494-8686, (Moderate), is also quite modern, but in a more subdued and elegant fashion. Beyond its expansive floor-to-ceiling windows, you'll discover a European-style restaurant enhanced by textured terra-cotta and beige walls, rustic tile, and bleached woods. The open mezzanine is a romantic and intimate place to enjoy provocative Italian cuisine.

LAS BRISAS, Laguna Beach
361 Cliff Drive
(714) 497-5434
Moderate

At the corner of Cliff Drive and the Pacific Coast Highway, just north of the main beach.

This is one of the few restaurants in Laguna Beach with a beguiling ocean vantage point, the major, if not only, reason for its inclusion. Not that the food isn't good Spanish cuisine and not that the restaurant isn't attractive, because they are: it's just too popular and bustling to be considered romantic. But the view makes up for all of that. From the outdoor patio you can watch the crashing white water and swirling eddies that explode over the rocks below. When sunset nears, a single path of sunlight graces the water's surface, and then, slowly, the collage of color crescendoes into nightfall while you ponder where the evening will take you next.

◆   **Romantic Note:** If sitting in a restaurant cramps your afternoon aspirations, stretch your legs in the well-maintained ocean-view park just north of Las Brisas.

LE PETIT GOURMET, Laguna Beach
332 Forest Avenue
(714) 494-5156
Inexpensive to Moderate

The restaurant is on the north side of the street, upstairs in a small shopping plaza.

Part of the fun of coming to Laguna Beach is winding your way through all the shops, restaurants, and art galleries. It seems that behind every colorful boutique is another intriguing nook or cranny offering something you can't live without. Working your way through the maze you will be delighted you happened upon this little restaurant.

What makes Le Petit Gourmet so appealing is that it's romantic without really trying. The atmosphere is casual, yet elegant, an eclectic mix of rustic French country and modern high-tech. On the walls, twigs and vines entwined with tiny white lights adorn the windows, entrance, and small mirrored alcove. Fortunately, the food is just as pleasing. Breakfast includes such tempting dishes as avocado benedict, Belgian waffles smothered with strawberries, and fresh-baked gingerbread served with a creme Chantilly. The lunch menu includes a variety of quiches, gourmet salads, and delicious and healthful sandwiches. A favorite is the curried chicken sandwich made with raisins, coconut, and apple, served with soup or salad. Le Petit Gourmet also serves dinner during the summer tourist season—accompanied on weekends by live music on the patio—but it's worth the trip to come here any time of year, even if you're just after a cup of mocha.

MONIQUE'S RESTAURANT, Laguna Beach
31727 Pacific Coast Highway
(714) 499-5359
Moderate

On the corner of Pacific Coast Highway and 3rd Street.

When it comes to romance, Monique's meets all the criteria. The interior is reminiscent of a plush provincial home, trimmed in lace, brimming with candlelight, and set high above the ocean. The entrees are mouth-watering and the portions generous; the waiters are considerate and accommodating. On quiet nights, customers are seated in secluded corners and may feel as though they have the place to themselves. There are four small dining areas to choose from, each with a warmth all its own. You can choose to dine on the garden patio or by the light of the hearth, but more sparks seem to fly in the tiny rooms that overlook the sea.

STUDIO MILANO, Laguna Beach
480 South Pacific Coast Highway
(714) 494-3093
Inexpensive to Moderate

Just a few blocks south of the main beach on the South Pacific Coast Highway.

Studio Milano is the type of place that makes you do a double take: something about its open, airy dining room, marbled terra-cotta walls, and sprinkling of tiny tables lures you beyond its threshold in search of answers. Yes, the savory Italian food lives up to its surroundings. Yes, sunsets on the water can be seen from the window tables looking out onto the highway and in the mirrored wall extending across the back of the restaurant. And yes, in summer the brick courtyard is a popular place for lovers to dine and toast the fact that they didn't pass this one by.

THE TERRACE RESTAURANT, Laguna Beach
448 South Pacific Coast Highway
(714) 497-4441
Inexpensive to Moderate

The Terrace is about two blocks south of the beach on a walkway called Peppertree Lane. It's marked by a wrought-iron gate directly across the street from the Hotel Laguna.

One day as I was trying to avoid the Laguna Beach tourist crunch, I happened to turn onto a small shopping walkway directly off the main drag. I found myself in the middle of a quaint row of shops catering specifically to the senses: one with a dizzying display of gourmet chocolates, another devoted to fragrant soaps and perfumes. Then I spotted a brass railing winding its way up a mysterious staircase. As I climbed to the top I was startled by what I saw. The Terrace Restaurant is built around a large tree, which literally sprawls through the dining area and up through the roof. The result is a luxurious treehouse with abundant greenery, and blossoming with pink tablecloths and candlelight. On top of all that, the food is good and reasonably priced.

◆   **Romantic Note: PARTNER'S BISTRO**, downstairs from The Terrace, is run by the same owners. Although it is darker and more stately than The Terrace, the bistro also has its romantic side and shares much of the same menu.

VILLAGE MARKET RESTAURANT, Laguna Beach
577 South Pacific Coast Highway
(714) 494-6344
Inexpensive to Moderate

About a quarter mile south of the main beach, near the intersection of Legion and South Pacific Coast Highway.

Perched on an ocean bluff in the heart of the city is a series of small shops where those with creative skills sell their wares. This is also the stimulating location of The Village Market Restaurant, a cliffside terrace where local musicians perform as you sip wine, talk over the day's events, and peruse the glistening shoreline. Unfortunately, the menu isn't very exciting and the food is rather simple, but what the meals lack is easily made up for by a view that is nothing less than sublime.

◆ **Romantic Warning**: Seating is on a first-come, first-served basis. With only 18 small tables, that can mean a long wait, especially at sunset.

Outdoor Kissing

CRESCENT BAY POINT PARK, Laguna Beach
After you reach Laguna Beach on the Pacific Coast Highway, turn west onto Crescent Bay Drive. A sign points the way to the park.

In an otherwise quiet, affluent suburban neighborhood (where you suspect the residents would rather not have you cruising by), this marvelous park arches out over the Pacific, crisscrossed by multilevel walkways. Cliff-edge belvederes provide fine views. Here sunset splashes colors onto the sky in shades of gold, amber, red, and violet that are astonishing in their intensity. This is the place to throw a blanket onto the ground and linger over a loaf of bread, a jug of wine, and thou.

Dana Point

Hotel/Bed and Breakfast Kissing

BLUE LANTERN INN, Dana Point
34343 Street of the Blue Lantern
(714) 661-1304
Moderate to Unbelievably Expensive

One block west of the Pacific Coast Highway on Street of the Blue Lantern.

The Blue Lantern Inn was built and is managed by the Four Sisters Inn Corporation, a group that knows everything there is to know about creating romantic accommodations. All of their bed and breakfasts—they also run The White Swan Inn and Petite Auberge in San Francisco, The Green Gables Inn and Gosby House in Pacific Grove, and The Cobblestone Inn in Carmel—are stunning, plush places to get away from it all.

The inn is located on a bluff overlooking the incredible California coastline; each of the 29 rooms has its own fireplace, Jacuzzi tub, ministereo system, fluffy terrycloth robes, a comfortable bed overflowing with pillows, and sweeping views. Enjoy a gourmet breakfast on your own private sun deck, along with an ocean breeze and a glistening surf. They also offer afternoon tea in the library by the hearth. At night your bed is turned down and chocolates left next to a teddy bear with a card that reads, "Good-night. Sleep tight. Don't let the bears bite." A little corny, but definitely endearing. This just may be one of the best places to kiss on the coast of Southern California.

THE CALIFORNIAN, Dana Point
24532 Del Prado
(714) 661-1001, (800) 432-2201
Very Expensive

Call for directions.

If the two of you share a love of the ocean, why not take your passion on the road, or to be more accurate, to the high seas? The Nautical Heritage Society of Dana Point offers charters to romantic California ports of call aboard *The Californian*, a replica of the first Coast Guard vessel to come to the West Coast in 1849. If you're picturing lounging around the boat all day, I'm afraid you've got the wrong idea. This is a hands-on experience, where participants work closely with the crew to learn how to sail and navigate the boat. The accommodations are cozy but simple, unless you splurge and go for the Governor's Cabin, which features two private staterooms, shower, pantry, library, and fireplace. And while this floating bed and breakfast may not be for everyone, it could provide an unforgettable adventure for couples drawn by the romance of the sea.

DANA POINT RESORT, Dana Point
25135 Park Lantern
(800) 533-9748, (714) 661-5000
Moderate to Unbelievably Expensive

From Dana Point Harbor Drive, go west until you reach Park Lantern and turn right.

Take an elegant, upscale hotel, mix in a touch of Disney magic, and you've got the Dana Point Resort. This Cape Cod-style resort has more than a bit of fairy tale about it. Like a great castle, it is set on a grassy knoll high above the sea, blushing in soft pastels and brimming with bright flowers. After the valet takes your car, the doorman greets you, and the concierge offers her undying devotion, you can't help but feel like royalty. So why not live like royalty? After a lazy afternoon of lounging in the pool, playing tennis, or enjoying a massage in the Health Spa, you can wander down to the lobby where afternoon tea is graciously served with an ocean view. As the pianist croons love songs, your tuxedoed waiter will tempt you with one indulgent sweet after another. Go ahead, give in.

When it comes to dining, you'll love the resort's restaurant, **WATER-COLORS**, which accents splashes of color with white wicker furniture. It looks out onto lovely gardens and has a sweeping view of the shoreline, making it an ideal location for a romantic candlelight dinner or a festive Sunday brunch. The end to a perfect day, or the beginning of a perfect night, may come when you share a quiet moment on your private seaside terrace and survey the moonlit domain lying before you.

RITZ CARLTON LAGUNA NIGUEL, Dana Point
33533 Ritz-Carlton Drive
(714) 240-2000
Very Expensive to Unbelievably Expensive

Take the Crown Valley Parkway exit from Interstate 5 and head west. Turn left on Pacific Coast Highway and proceed one mile to Ritz Carlton Drive. Turn right on Ritz Carlton Drive; the entrance will be on your left.

"Luxurious" doesn't begin to describe the Ritz Carlton: the hotel is lavish, opulent, and very expensive. Actually, how much you spend here is up to you. For example, you can reserve the Presidential Suite ($2,000) or you can just drop by for a drink and sunset viewing at the oceanfront lounge (about $10). The romantic possibilities are endless.

The hotel is like a grand white castle perched on an ocean bluff. You can be assured that those who stay here get the royal treatment; there are two employees for every guest room. The rooms are comfortable and attractive, decorated in pleasant pastels. Those with the best views command the highest tariffs. Guests have a free rein on the tennis courts, in the crystal-clear swimming pools, and at the fitness center, golf course, specialty shops, and beauty salon. But you don't have to be a guest to enjoy the lovely restaurants, or to take afternoon tea in the library filled with rare antique books or the posh lobby area with its silk-lined walls, overstuffed couches, and grand, comfortable chairs. From this vantage point you can gaze over rousing ocean views and partake in stimulating conversation. It's easy to talk words of love when you find a spot so provocative and intriguing.

Restaurant Kissing

THE CHART HOUSE, Dana Point
34443 Street of the Green Lantern
(714) 493-1183
Moderate to Expensive

Take the Pacific Coast Highway and go west on Street of the Blue Lantern.
Turn right on Santa Clara and left on Street of the Green Lantern.

I've tried to steer clear of chain restaurants while researching this book, because all too often they use a certain formula for romance and most of the time the formula falls flat.

But this is one restaurant that can't be ignored. Its view is just too exhilarating, its dining rooms too inviting. Located at the pinnacle of Dana Point, the Chart House enjoys a view that stretches all the way from its harbor, teeming with boats, to the San Diego shore. After spiraling down the staircase to reach its main floor, you'll come upon several circular dining rooms, each embellished by jewel-tone booths, exotic flowers, and astonishing ocean vistas. The aroma of seafood adds to the feeling that you've discovered seaside rapture, though the menu offers plenty of tasty meat and pasta dishes as well. Although there isn't a bad table in the house, you may want to stroll on the terrace before or after your meal to get the full effect of this incredible mountaintop vista. Breathtaking.

◆   **Romantic Alternative: CANNONS**, 34344 Street of the Green Lantern, Dana Point, (714) 496-6146, (Moderate to Expensive), is also located on an enviable piece of real estate—high on a mountain cliff, a lone rampart over the coastline—with views that are simply stupendous. The entire dining room is decorated in sky-inspired pastels and encircled by floor-to-ceiling windows that showcase everything south and due west. Sunset from here is an unforgettable experience. The spectrum of colors on the horizon, along the shore, and on the slopes of the mountainside is phenomenal. I wish I could say that the food is as fantastic as the view, but with such competition from Mother Nature, why even bother? Still, you won't be disappointed, and the service is friendly and relaxed.

Outdoor Kissing

LANTERN BAY PARK, Dana Point

From Dana Park Harbor Road, turn right on Park Lantern and follow it to the top of the hill.

This is one of the most romantic spots in the area, with a breath-taking view. Memories of any time spent on its turf with someone you love will be richly treasured.

◆   **Romantic Alternative**: Sandwiched between the Ritz Carlton and a scattering of exclusive estates is **SALT CREEK BEACH PARK**, a hillside stretch of lawn with a million-dollar view. A popular spot for surfing, it's also a great place to marvel at the splendor around you. Ritz guests can take a garden walkway to the park. Those who have come by car can park in the large metered lot off Pacific Coast Highway and meander down.

Capistrano

Hotel/Bed and Breakfast Kissing

CAPISTRANO SEASIDE INN, Capistrano Beach   ◆◀
34862 Pacific Coast Highway
(714) 496-1399
Inexpensive

At the corner of Palisades and Old Highway 1.

At the time this edition went to press the Seaside Capistrano Inn was undergoing fairly extensive renovations, so we can't comment on the new interior. However, what makes this bed and breakfast so appealing is the fact that every room has a fireplace, a private patio, and a garden or ocean view. The grounds of this 1930s Spanish-style inn are filled with flowers and foliage, and the beach is just across the street

The inn is located on a very busy street corner, which probably explains its remarkably inexpensive prices. The noise does subside at night, and with so much for so little (the view is wondrous) this is a bargain kissing place.

Restaurant Kissing

L'HIRONDELLE, Capistrano
31631 Camino Capistrano
(714) 661-0425
Moderate

From Interstate 5, take the Ortega Highway and go west. Turn right at Camino Capistrano.

Just across from the famed San Juan Capistrano Mission is a restaurant with a mission all its own: to be the source of romantic inspiration for anyone who crosses its threshold. Mission accomplished. Quaint, charming, and decidedly French, L'Hirondelle combines European country elegance with a sense of humor. Along with the lace curtains, crisp white linens, fresh flowers, and candlelight, you'll find a delightful melange of knickknacks and curios. The walls and shelves are overflowing with old plates, hats, pots, and dolls. Conversation pieces, maybe, but the real topic here is the cuisine extraordinare. Better yet, why talk at all, when you can feast on cherries jubilee and steal a few sinfully sweet kisses.

Outdoor Kissing

PINES PARK, Capistrano Beach

Take Highway 101 to Palisades and head inland. At Camino Capistrano, turn right. The park is about a half mile up the road, on your right.

Set on a bluff high above the ocean, Pines Park has views that are intoxicating. You may feel a bit giddy as you spread out a blanket on the vividly green lawn, peer out at the sun-sequinned ocean below, and listen to the symphony of waves as they crash against the shore. You can certainly do some momentous kissing here.

San Clemente

Hotel/Bed and Breakfast Kissing

CASA DE FLORES, San Clemente
184 Avenida la Cuesta
(714) 498-1344
Inexpensive to Moderate

Call for directions.

If you'd like to stay at a bed and breakfast with a personal touch, consider this delightful San Clemente casa. True to its name, the attractive Spanish-style home is bedecked with colorful bougainvillea and other assorted flora. Though it's a few miles from the sea, this hillside abode has a lovely view of the coastline, especially from a guest chamber lovingly named Suite Memories. This room comes with a private bath, fireplace, and its own enclosed courtyard complete with hot tub. The other room, Tea for Two, has a California king-size bed, a private bath, a lush backyard view, and a small sitting area that provided the inspiration for its name. Both suites have a TV and VCR, and upstairs you'll find a family room filled with more than 300 videos to choose from. A stay here includes a robust gourmet breakfast, free use of the pool table, and an owner who is happy to act as a golf partner should one of you wish to pick up the clubs.

CASA TROPICANA, San Clemente
610 Avenida Victoria
(714) 492-1234
Moderate to Unbelievably Expensive

From Interstate 5, take the El Camino Real exit and go west. Turn left on Del Mar to the pier. Casa Tropicana is just across the street.

If your taste runs to the tropical or the exotic and you yearn for a room with an astonishing ocean view, welcome to paradise!

This unusual inn, set above the San Clemente pier, offers a tremendous vista of the sparkling Pacific. Each of the nine guest chambers follows a tropical or jungle theme, from the Bogie-and-Bacall-inspired *Key Largo* to the romantic *Out of Africa*, complete with four-poster bed draped in mosquito netting. A couple of the rooms carried the theme a little too far for my taste (the ceiling of the *Emerald Forest* is entirely covered with vines and the *Bali Hai* will make you feel like you should be drinking something with an umbrella in it), but maybe there's something to be said for fulfilling those *Me Tarzan, you Jane* fantasies. Most rooms have fireplaces and Jacuzzi bathtubs, and two of the three suites have complete kitchenettes, ideal for an extended getaway. But if you really want to take a trip to Fantasy Island, consider splurging on the exquisite penthouse. Elegantly decorated, this gorgeous suite has its own sun deck, a 180-degree ocean view, and a seductive wraparound fireplace accessible to both the master bedroom and the Jacuzzi.

The Casa Tropicana has a small restaurant on the first floor that also follows the tropical theme. In the morning, you can choose from one of the breakfast entrees on its menu and dine on the terrace or in the privacy of your own room. Across the street you'll find a small ocean-vista park, perfect for picnicking.

◆ **Romantic Warning:** You can take the train to a stop nearby. The bad news is that this same train passes right by the hotel hourly.

◆ **Romantic Suggestion:** A walk on the pier is a must, and while you're there why not stop for a bite at **THE FISHERMAN'S**

RESTAURANT AND BAR, 611 Avenida Victoria, San Clemente, (714) 498-6390, (Inexpensive to Moderate), for great clam chowder and fresh fish dishes. You can reel in a spectacular sunset almost every night.

Restaurant Kissing

ETIENNE'S, San Clemente
215 South El Camino Real
(714) 492-7263
Moderate to Unbelievably Expensive

From Interstate 5, take the South El Camino Real turnoff and travel north for one mile.

Looking somewhat like a Spanish hacienda on the outside and a French country cottage on the inside, Etienne's is a restaurant of curious contradictions. Its interior has a simple, unpretentious feeling—lace curtains, open beamed ceiling, and modest antiques—yet the ambience is a little stuffy and the service a bit pretentious. But if you can overlook that and find a quiet corner or window table to call your own, you can find a chance for romance. Chateaubriand for two, a bottle of fine French wine, and some loving conversation whispered across the table will surely make your evening.

"*Press yourself into a drop of wine, and pour yourself into the purest flame.*"

Rainer Maria Rilke

"It's overdoing the thing to die of love."
Anonymous

CATALINA ISLAND

Two hours from the mainland, 22 miles out in the Pacific, is a little bit of Hawaii called Catalina, with 54 miles of shoreline. And what a shoreline this is, with countless hidden beaches, rugged cliffs, endless hiking trails, and abundant marine life that includes whales during their yearly migration. Most of the soaring countryside is a deep lustrous green, and the island is invigorating, unpopulated, and remarkably smog-free. When you leave the ferry, you're in the port of Avalon, a seaside European-style town replete with adorable restaurants, sidewalk cafes, and charming accommodations.

One of the more-becoming commercial aspects of this illustrious port of call is that transient cars are not allowed; the dominant forms of wheeled transportation on the island are bikes and motor scooters. Those of you from the mainland who feel more married to your automobiles than to your mates will find leaving the car behind a welcome change. The *Catalina Express* is the fastest way there by water; if you want to get there even quicker, helicopter excursions are available. Whichever way you go, it is our heartfelt conclusion that a visit to Catalina is a Southern California romantic must. Put simply, Catalina is paradise!

◆ **Romantic Note:** **CATALINA CRUISES**, (213) 253-9800, is located at the San Pedro Catalina Terminal. Cruise reservations are required and rates vary by season; some boats are based at the New Catalina Landing, located in downtown Long Beach. **CATALINA HOLIDAY PASSENGER SERVICE** offers cruises from Balboa Pavilion at Newport Beach, (714) 673-5245. **CATALINA EXPRESS**, (213) 519-1212, offers daily, year-round departures from San Pedro and seasonal service from Redondo Beach. Before you make any firm decisions, call the Catalina Chamber of Commerce, (213) 510-1520, for brochures on accommodations, restaurants, and sports equipment rentals. It is one of the most hospitable chambers of commerce you are likely to run into anywhere.

Hotel/Bed and Breakfast Kissing

THE INN ON MOUNT ADA, Avalon
Catalina Island
398 Wrigley Road
(310) 510-2030
Very Expensive to Unbelievably Expensive

All the cabs know the way, so just leave it to them or wait for the inn's transfer shuttle. Once you arrive you will have use of your own golf cart.

Traveling to Catalina Island is like embarking on a romantic fantasy. As I waited to board the ferry, I visualized myself crossing the Mediterranean, en route to a torrid tryst at a villa on the Riviera. The speed of the boat was matched by my increasing anticipation as the mainland blurred into hues of azure, jade, and slate. When the ferry docked, I knew the start of my weekend adventure was only moments away and soon my anticipation would give way to reality. For those of us who like to get carried away and don't want to bother with passports or air fares, the Inn on Mount Ada offers a convenient substitute for a villa on the Riviera.

The Inn on Mount Ada was once the Wrigley Mansion and, believe me, the Wrigleys knew how to live. The massive white structure, perched on a hilltop overlooking a sweeping view of the island, contains six superbly remodeled suites upstairs, all with exquisite views and absolutely perfect everything else. Downstairs you have access to all possible amenities of opulent living. Yes, it's pricey, but just think about what a memorable weekend you can have here.

◆ **Romantic Alternatives**: Catalina offers more than 30 hotel and bed-and-breakfast establishments. These four are our favorites.

GARDEN HOUSE INN, 125 Clarissa, Avalon, Catalina Island, (310) 510-0356, (Moderate to Unbelievably Expensive), represents the best of what a traditional bed and breakfast is supposed to be. The innkeepers here know what it means to pamper their guests. Their advice and courtesies are superb. All of the nine rooms are exceedingly comfortable and quaint, replete with handmade quilts, floral wallpaper, and cushy sofas and chairs; some have private decks, terraces, and views. The breakfast is continental but generous, and the rooftop sun deck gives sightseeing a whole new dimension.

GLENMORE PLAZA HOTEL, 120 Sumner Avenue, Avalon, Catalina Island, (213) 510-0017, (Moderate to Expensive), is one of the most well-known spots on the island, and its reputation is well deserved. In bygone days the Glenmore Hotel was famous for its glittering Hollywood clientele. Now it hosts eager couples looking to escape from the world at large. The airy and bright rooms are filled with wicker, the cushy beds are covered with down comforters, and the whirlpool baths promote soapy relaxation. The beach is directly across the street.

GULL HOUSE BED AND BREAKFAST, 344 Whittley Avenue, Avalon, Catalina Island, (310) 510-2547, (Inexpensive), is probably as intimate as bed and breakfasts get. Of the four guest rooms here two are suites. With more than 600 square feet of relaxing room, these suites include a private living room with a fireplace and a morning breakfast nook. Guests are welcome on the outdoor patio, which has a tiled pool, a spa, and a gas barbecue available for use. The furnishings are more contemporary than cozy, but the space and the privacy more than make up for that minor flaw.

THE OLD TURNER INN, 223 Catalina Avenue, Avalon, Catalina Island, (310) 510-2236, (Moderate to Expensive), is set in the heart of Avalon, the main town of Catalina Island. The handsomely renovated interior is simple but lovely, and the rooms are gracious and serene. Most of the suites have wood-burning fireplaces, private outside patios, and plenty of radiant sunshine streaming in through the windows.

"For a moment each seemed unreal to the other... then the slow warm hum of love began."
F. Scott Fitzgerald

LAKE ARROWHEAD AND BIG BEAR LAKE

LAKE ARROWHEAD, BIG BEAR LAKE

From Interstate 10 or Interstate 15 East, follow the signs to Highway 18. Then follow the signs to Lake Arrowhead.

Whoever wrote about "purple mountains' majesty above the fruited plains" must have had in mind the stunning scenery that follows the World Highway 18 north from San Bernardino to Big Bear Lake. As you climb to 6,700 feet above sea level, your eyes will revel in the scenic stimulation this region provides. From the time you leave the arid flatlands and begin your coiling climb up the road, you'll behold tableaus of granite-etched peaks and alpine greenery, as refreshing as they are wondrous. Not surprisingly, Big Bear and Lake Arrowhead were once the domain of Hollywood notables and their wealthy cohorts. Now this four-star resort area attracts vacationers who want to wake up in the mountains, eat in interesting restaurants, and stop in quaint boutiques between bursts of outdoor recreation.

Big Bear Lake and its environs are more pristine and rustic than the Lake Arrowhead area. Big Bear offers sensational camping experiences during the summer and exhilarating downhill skiing during the winter. Both are beautiful areas in which to rest your city-weary souls in Mother Nature's healing mountain air and scenery. Any time of year, you would be remiss if you didn't come here for blissful outdoor escapades.

Hotel/Bed and Breakfast Kissing

THE CARRIAGE HOUSE, Lake Arrowhead
472 Emerald Drive
(714) 336-1400
Inexpensive to Moderate

From the entrance to the village, follow Highway 173 to the second Emerald Drive.

Who said Grandma's country home is lost to us forever? At the Carriage House, you can easily recapture the simple pleasures of life in surroundings romantic and sweet. This is the kind of place where memories are made and savored for years to come.

Standing guard in front of this lovely New England-style inn is a 1902 doctor's carriage trimmed in twinkling white lights. The rooms follow this theme; each is named after a type of carriage: Brougham, Surrey, and Victoria. All are sigh provoking, decorated with delightful special touches. Featherbeds, cozy down comforters, braided rugs, rocking chairs, claw-foot tubs, window seats looking out to the lake, and large family-style breakfasts combine to create a feeling of *deja vu*. Haven't you been here before? Yes—in your dreams of the perfect romantic retreat.

CHATEAU DU LAC, Lake Arrowhead
911 Hospital Road
(714) 337-6488
Moderate to Unbelievably Expensive

Take Highway 173 to Hospital Road. The Chateau is up the hill on your right.

This bed and breakfast has one undeniable special attraction: it peers down onto the lake. Surely this is one reason that Chateau du Lac was proclaimed "Bed and Breakfast of the Month" by *Country Inn* magazine—a prestigious honor indeed.

It's easy to understand, though. Gingerbread on the outside, fairy tale on the inside, this magnificent inn has it all. It's elegant without being pretentious, romantic without being frothy, and let's not forget that to-die-for view. Each of the six guest rooms is expertly appointed, with a stuffed animal here and a throw pillow there to give them a welcoming touch. Though incredibly expensive, the Lakeview Suite is worth going into hock for. I can just imagine winter here, sipping brandy in bed and gazing out at the snow-topped mountains as a fire crackles softly on the hearth. Warm summer nights could be spent enjoying the private Jacuzzi and gazing out onto the moonlit lake, the lights of the town dancing upon it.

Breakfast is served on the terrace or in the formal dining room. Expect to be treated to homemade egg dishes, scones, quiches, omeletes, and/ or other gourmet treats. Afternoon tea is also a lavish affair. But if you're going to have a lavish affair, this is the place to have it.

EAGLE'S LANDING, Lake Arrowhead
27406 Cedarwood
(714) 336-2642
Moderate to Expensive

Take North Bay Drive to Cedarwood; Eagle's Landing is on the corner.

Eagle's Landing is a modern mountain inn set in an exclusive West Shore neighborhood. Unlike the many frilly bed and breakfasts located in this neck of the woods, Eagle's Landing has a more masculine feeling. The four guest rooms are decorated primarily in earth tones. The spectacular Lake View Suite enjoys a rustic early California-style decor. By far the inn's most romantic offering, the suite has a sitting room, large bath, full bar, wood-burning fireplace, TV, refrigerator, and just about everything you could need to burrow in and hibernate together for days. From its private terrace you can appreciate a panoramic view of the lake, sparkling by day, reflecting the stars by night.

When morning arrives, so does a hearty country breakfast. Afternoon hors d'oeuvres are complimentary. A large, comfy hammock beneath the pines awaits your indulgence.

THE GOLD MOUNTAIN MANOR, Big Bear City
1117 Anita
(714) 585-6997
Inexpensive to Expensive

Call for directions.

If you're looking for a romantic mountain hideaway, it really doesn't get much better than this. The astutely renovated mansion contains seven exceptional suites, each with a character all its own. What the rooms have in common are wood-burning fireplaces and antique furnishings. Breakfast is a tantalizing affair that will keep you going strong on a morning hike through the national forest, one block down the road. Hors d'oeuvres are served at 5 P.M.

THE KNICKERBOCKER MANSION, Big Bear Lake
869 South Knickerbocker
(714) 866-8221
Moderate to Expensive

Take Big Bear Boulevard to Knickerbocker and head south.

Have you ever seen a snow globe? First you shake it, then you watch in delight as fluffy snowflakes dance around a rustic mountain scene. If your answer is yes, then you have some idea of the kind of winter-fantasy-come-true that awaits you at The Knickerbocker Mansion. But there's romance to be found here year-round. This enormous log cabin was built in the 1920s at the base of the San Bernardino National Forest. Just blocks from town, it's privy to the best of both worlds: the quiet and solitude of the woods, and the lure of Big Bear's quaint shops and restaurants.

The Knickerbocker Mansion has been described as what the Ponderosa might have looked like if Ben Cartwright's wife had survived the birth of Little Joe. I couldn't have said it better myself. The inn is rustic yet cozy, with a few feminine touches here and there. The sitting room contains a scattering of Victorian antiques and comfortable couches and chairs; its grandfather clock serves to remind you that you've come to a place where time seems to pass a bit more slowly, the days lasting a bit longer. Follow your nose to Grandma's kitchen, where you'll find cider brewing and the cookie jar open. Help yourself to the coffee, tea, and chocolate kisses as well.

The main house holds four guest rooms, three with shared bath, and a large "treetop" suite with potbellied stove, TV/VCR, and Jacuzzi. Four additional loft rooms with private baths are located in the restored carriage house next door. The rooms aren't exactly luxurious: lived-in is more accurate, and in some ways is actually praise. Here you feel like you're visiting with close friends who have tidied up and brought out the best linens for you. The result is a place where you can find total contentment and romantic repose.

◆ **Romantic Alternative: THE EAGLE'S NEST,** 41675 Big Bear Boulevard, Big Bear Valley, (714) 866-6465, (Inexpensive to Very Expensive), is also quite rustic, but has a much more Western flair (as in bang-bang-shoot-em-up Western). This is definitely for the couple who prefers log walls to lily-of-the-valley wallpaper. There are four rooms in the main house and three cottage suites. Each is named after a Western movie, as stained glass insets in the bathroom doors will remind you. Not romantic, you say? You'd be surprised. All of the cottage suites have a fireplace, and the Annie Oakley has a Jacuzzi strategically placed near the hearth. Happy trails.

ROMANTIQUE LAKEVIEW LODGE, Lake Arrowhead ◆◆◆
28051 Highway 189
(800) 358-5253
Inexpensive to Expensive

Across from Lake Arrowhead Village, in the heart of Lake Arrowhead.

From the moment you scale the steps to the lodge's lovely front terrace, set high above the shimmering lake, you can't help but anticipate the night ahead. Elegant Victorian furnishings and a blazing hearth in the beautifully appointed lobby add to the feeling that you've discovered someplace exceptionally special.

Each of the eight rooms seems to perfectly unite old-world charm with modern comforts. Antiques, lace curtains, fireplaces, luxurious private baths, and panoramic lake views are just some of what you'll find here. And while TVs and VCRs tend to detract from romance more than add to it, the thought of curling up with a steamy classic on a snowy night sounds pretty darned *romantique*.

◆ **Romantic Suggestion**: If you'd like a heartier breakfast than the continental one served at the lodge—or if you just have a sweet tooth—follow your nose to the **BELGIAN WAFFLE WORKS**, dockside at Lake Arrowhead Village, (714) 337-5222, (Inexpensive), for mouth-watering waffles served a multitude of delicious ways. This petite country-style restaurant is situated right along the shore and in high season scoring a window seat may be difficult. Take heart: they add a few terrace tables in the summer, ideal for taking in the view, the food, and some maple-flavored kisses.

◆ **Additional Romantic Suggestion**: After breakfast consider taking a cruise on the **ARROWHEAD QUEEN**, LeRoy's Sports, (714) 866-7574. This Mississippi-style paddleboat leaves once an hour and gives you a narrated tour of picturesque Lake Arrowhead.

SADDLEBACK INN, Lake Arrowhead
300 South Highway 173
(714) 336-3571, (800) 858-3334
Moderate to Expensive

On South Highway 173, at the entrance to Lake Arrowhead Village.

This rather elegant inn offers 10 rooms in the main building and a handful of chalets scattered over three acres. The rooms in the lodge, each lovingly draped with pastel country fabrics, are the most desirable for your mountain retreat; all contain built-for-two spa tubs and very comfortable furnishings. The inn is situated at the entrance to Lake Arrowhead Village, which is convenient but not exactly remote. (Sometimes you have to sacrifice one detail for another when it comes to heart-tugging accommodations.) There is also a charming restaurant at the inn, open for breakfast, lunch, and dinner.

STORYBOOK INN, Sky Forest
28717 Highway 18
(714) 336-1483
Moderate to Very Expensive

On Highway 18 near the Kuffel Canyon turnoff in the city of Sky Forest (three miles or so from Lake Arrowhead).

Depending on your point of view, you will either think this inn is a place to fall in love all over again or somewhat overpriced and slightly in need of repairs. One thing everyone will agree on is the view. This three-story mansion rests at the edge of a mountain cliff and on clear days you can practically see forever (about 100 miles). There are nine rooms and a somewhat rustic cabin to chose from, all with private baths and a few with glass-enclosed patios or porches. Each room is named after a book or fairy tale, with a dog-eared copy of the story occupying a special place of honor. The best suite is *Gone With The Wind*, a vivid confection of Laura Ashley floral prints, complete with a private solarium and spectacular mountain view. The inn offers not only a full gourmet breakfast, but evening hors d'oeuvres and chocolate chip cookies and milk before bed. A dip in the bubbling, hot outdoor Jacuzzi could be the perfect end to a chilly day.

◆   **Romantic Suggestion: HEAP'S PEAK ARBORETUM**, about a half mile down the highway, is a beautiful walking trail ideal for learning about the splendors of nature. As sunlight streams through the pines, you'll discover pockets of wildflowers, rare plants, lots of wild creatures, and a wonderfully melodic brook. Placards along the circular path reveal little-known facts about the lush forest life around you. Best of all, the trail is only three-quarters of a mile long, and easy enough for even the least ambitious hikers.

◆   **Romantic Alternative**: Halfway between the Storybook Inn and Lake Arrowhead, you'll find the **SKY FOREST BED AND BREAKFAST INN**, 760 Kuffel Canyon Road, Sky Forest, (714) 337-4680, (800) 339-3368, (Moderate to Expensive). Though it doesn't have the Storybook Inn's incredible view, this lovely mountain estate is nestled among the pine and dogwood trees and has a marvelous country feeling.

The house is large and modern and each of its five rooms has a high wood-beamed ceiling with skylight. Your stay comes with a full breakfast and you certainly won't want to miss the nightly wine and hors d'oeuvres served downstairs by the flickering fire.

WILLOW CREEK INN, Lake Arrowhead
1176 North Highway 173
(714) 336-2008, (800) 834-6415
Moderate to Expensive

On the north side of Lake Arrowhead on North Highway 173, or follow North Bay Road around the lake until it turns into Highway 173.

When you leave the Willow Creek Inn, you will promptly yearn to turn back and spend more time walking along the forested grounds. Willow Creek, a new bed and breakfast, occupies a rambling Cape Cod-style mansion. It has an open airy feeling, no doubt due to the pastel color scheme, white-washed woods, and abundance of windows escalating to the very high vaulted ceiling. Upstairs the guest rooms are decorated with a great deal of care. In *Hearts and Flowers* you'll find plenty of both, as well as a king-size brass bed covered with an Amish heart quilt, Victorian oak antiques, and an engaging window seat. The focal point of the Four Poster is its feather-nest bed overflowing with pillows, while the *Sunrise Room* is a treat for the eyes in vivid Laura Ashley prints. The most romantic accommodation, though, is the *Honeymoon Suite.* Separated from the other rooms for maximum privacy, it claims its own entrance, fireplace, terrace, and an unforgettable mountain view. Add to that a double Jacuzzi tub sharing this panoramic vista and you've got a measure of Eden in the forest.

I should also mention the private baths, the color TVs, the exercise room, the hammock lazily hung between shade trees, and the boat rides along the lake with the owners. With all that Willow Creek has to offer, it's easy to miss something. But whatever you do, don't miss the gourmet breakfast: heart-shaped waffles, apple pancakes, omelets, Scandinavian aebleskivers, or other delectable dishes are likely to make their way onto your plates.

WINDY POINT INN, Fawnskin

39263 North Shore Drive
(714) 866-2746
Expensive to Unbelievably Expensive

Follow Highway 138 (North Shore Drive) to Fawnskin.

Mountain lore has it that a young, handsome man stricken with a terminal illness devoted his last days to building a place so beautiful, so compelling, so intimate that no romantic could resist. Like the director of a great love story he proceeded to set the stage. First he found the land, a beautiful secluded point along a glistening azure lake. Though it was not for sale, he convinced the owners to sell and allow him his dream. He then found the best craftsmen, and with no more than the ideas in his head he expertly designed and decorated the tranquil oasis now known as the Windy Point Inn.

This is the only bed and breakfast in Big Bear set directly upon the shore, and it's easy to see how that fact directly influenced the inn's design. Everywhere you look you'll find window seats, private decks, everything and anything to help take in the incredible views. The decor is elegant and sophisticated, combining high-tech, rustic antiques, and eclectic pieces of art. Nowhere is this better illustrated than in *The Peaks*, the very expensive but unbelievably luxurious master suite. Beyond romantic, it was designed so that no matter where you are in the suite, you can enjoy the dramatic lake views. Above your pillows, you'll find a strategically placed skylight that practically brings the stars into the bedroom. There's a fireplace in the corner, a sunken Jacuzzi tub, a double-headed-shower that doubles as a sauna, and a private deck with a tree growing right through it (after all, this is an environmentally protective resort).

In the morning, a full gourmet breakfast is served in the beautiful living room area by the blazing hearth. Listening to soft classical music and gazing out the wall of windows to a flawless lakefront view, you will probably feel the way that I did. Windy Point Inn must have been created by someone incredibly special.

◆   **Romantic Alternative: THE INN AT FAWNSKIN**, 880 Canyon, Fawnskin, (714) 866-3200, (Inexpensive to Expensive), is everything you'd envision a mountain getaway to be. This log mansion is a
great place to sip hot toddies by the fire after a long day of skiing. Better
yet, why not sink into the bubbling hot Jacuzzi? Though the rooms are
pretty simple, the master suite has a fireplace and a terrace with a lake
view. You can't ask for more than that.

Restaurant Kissing

CASUAL ELEGANCE, Agua Fria
26848 State Highway 189
(714) 337–8932
Moderate

In the center of Agua Fria, on Highway 189.

Whenever I asked the whereabouts of Lake Arrowhead's most romantic restaurant, I was always pointed in this direction. Located in the
center of a small mountain hamlet, this petite cottage is aglow in
candlelight and the brilliance of a glittering hearth. The dining rooms
are tiny—barely fitting three or four tables—so even when every chair
is filled, your need for intimacy is never threatened. Dinner is a long,
leisurely affair here, served in true French fashion with the salad served
last and sorbet between soup and entree. This gives you a chance to
enjoy your surroundings: the antiques, the lace curtains, the spotlighted
oil paintings. Better yet, it provides you with the opportunity to look
into your lover's eyes and savor an evening destined to be unforgettable.
◆   **Romantic Note:** It's difficult to say exactly what kind of cuisine
is served here because the menu changes weekly. Suffice it to say you will
find gourmet offerings of meat, seafood, fish, and pasta.
◆   **Romantic Suggestion:** Though you couldn't tell by its name,
THE IRON SQUIRREL, 646 Pine Knot Boulevard, Big Bear Lake,
(714) 866-9121, (Moderate to Expensive), has plenty of romantic
dining potential. Candlelight, dark woods, lace curtains, and sumptuous
French cuisine combine to create Big Bear's most intimate hideaway.

Across the street, you'll find another restaurant worth toasting to. **VINES**, 625 Pine Knot Boulevard, Big Bear Lake, (714) 866-3033, is owned by the Bear Valley Winery and has a small wine tasting bar attached to it. The restaurant is cheerfully romantic, mixing stark white with vivid floral and latticework prints. The ceiling even has real latticework wrapped with vines and faux grapes. Vines is located in an indoor marketplace that sells gourmet kitchen items and collectibles.

"When kisses are repeated and the arms hold
there is no telling where time is."
Ted Hughes

PALM SPRINGS

PALM SPRINGS

From Los Angeles: Take Interstate 10 east to Highway 111 into Palm Springs. From San Diego: Head north on Interstate 15, go east on Highway 60. Exit at Interstate 10 and go east to Highway 111.

I almost left Palm Springs out of my collection of kissing places. This man-made, concrete oasis is made up of straight slabs of highways and roads that crisscross vast stretches of overdeveloped, monotonous flatlands filled with trailer parks, suburban housing ventures, condominium complexes, shopping strips, spa resorts, hotels and motels, and jade green golf courses. Rising abruptly from this real estate explosion are the towering, rocky summits of the San Jacinto mountain range. The contrast between the natural rugged beauty of the land and the urban sprawl can be disconcerting. But for Californians (and ice-packed Midwesterners) who love their golf, heated fresh air, celebrity sightseeing, and outstanding resort accommodations, Palm Springs is more than an oasis—it's a spiritual sanctuary. Of course, the underlying reason for this fervent attachment to the desert is its sultry, omnipresent sunshine and abundant underground water supply. These wellsprings keep the developed areas green while the sun keeps everything else, for as far as the eye can see, burnished with tan, gold, and olive green. Although Palm Springs itself may not be romantic, it can be the setting for a literally heartwarming holiday.

Hotel/Bed and Breakfast Kissing

TWO BUNCH PALMS, Desert Hot Springs
67-425 Two Bunch Palms Trail
(619) 329-8791
Unbelievably Expensive

Only registered guests are allowed on the property. Before venturing here, call for directions.

Other resorts pale in comparison with this pinnacle of spa tranquillity and self-indulgence. (And I mean self-indulgence!) Guests check in for high-class pampering in one of the 44 private villas spread out on more than 100 lush, verdant, wooded acres. The villas, havens of bliss and comfort, are spacious, with plush furnishings and details. The stone-enclosed swimming pool is a fine place to splash together. And the restaurant, swathed in satiny golden hues cast by lovely stained glass windows, is an evocative setting for culinary and interpersonal magic.

Though all of this is enough for any two people who need time to do nothing, Two Bunch Palms is also a spa, and the services here will heal you mentally and physically. Options include side-by-side mud baths, body wraps, invigorating brush therapy, scalp massage, acupressure massage, reflexology of the hands and feet, and herbal steam baths. The variations and descriptions of these exquisite treatments sound as exotic as they feel, and can melt years of stress from every inch of your bodies. The sensations you'll take home with you after a few days here will last a long time.

VILLA ROYALE, Palm Springs
1620 Indian Trail
(619) 327-2314
Inexpensive to Expensive

From downtown Palm Springs, stay on North Palm Canyon Road, which becomes East Palm Canyon. At Indian Trail, turn left to the inn.

Talk about an oasis in the middle of an oasis! Villa Royale will make your hearts beat faster and cool your city-weary state of mind from the moment you arrive. This is rural grandeur with a luxuriant European flair. The 31 guest rooms, each with its own private entrance, front a series of inner courtyards enhanced by meandering brick paths, vine-covered stone arches, urns filled with flowering bushes, and bubbling stone fountains. Two swimming pools and a hot tub are hidden by towering palm tress. The rooms range from stunning to magnificent. No two are alike, but all are decorated in imported furnishings and fabrics, with firm, cushy beds and plush down comforters. Many of the suites have cozy sitting areas, stone fireplaces, french doors, and private patios and spas. There isn't a corner of this villa you won't find to be soothing and gracious.

◆ **Romantic Warning**: Villa Royale calls itself a bed and breakfast because of the continental morning meal served poolside in the center courtyard. The setting is undeniably romantic, but the service can be sparse and the food unappetizing. Not a great way to start a morning. At night the kitchen improves substantially, and the plush, rose-colored adobe dining room is the most attractive and intimate in all of Palm Springs.

◆ **Romantic Alternative: INGLESIDE INN**, 200 West Ramon Road, Palm Springs, (619) 325-0046, (Expensive to Unbelievably Expensive), promises to be everything you could want in an exclusive getaway in the heart of a world-famous resort. Unfortunately, that promise teeters on being slightly tacky. The guest suites encircle a lush garden that requires some manicuring. The rooms are lavishly decorated with period furnishings and some have fireplaces and private patios, but the poorly lit interiors are in need of remodeling and general sprucing up. Also, the bathrooms are dated and some of the furnishings could use recovering. What a shame that a place with such provocative possibilities (and high tariffs) can't seem to get its act together. Surely there is enough venture capital in town to handle a small project like this. With a little help, the Ingleside could be outstanding.

Outdoor Kissing

PALM SPRINGS AERIAL TRAMWAY, Palm Springs ❤❤❤
Highway 111 and Tramway Road
(619) 325-1391
$14.95 for adults roundtrip

Follow North Palm Canyon Road north out of town to Tramway Road. Turn left up the mountain to the tram.

This is the longest tramway in the world, which in itself is not a particularly moving (pun intended) statistic. The tourist concession stands are unimaginative and bleak. None of that, of course, has anything to do with kissing and tender moments. What has everything to do with snuggling close is the 15-minute, 12,800-foot ascent to perilous, rocky cliffs with astounding views and a temperature as much as 40 degrees below that of the desert floor. Here you'll find a winter wonderland of cross-country skiing and sledding, a summer paradise of endless hiking trails dusted with desert hues of gold and green, and the unsurpassed exhilaration that comes from being on top of the world. For the adventurous, camping facilities provide the ultimate in outdoor romance.

◆ **Romantic Warning:** This ride is not cheap. To really get full value from this stirring sightseeing attraction, come prepared to spend the day.

*"In real love you want the other person's good.
In romantic love you want the other person."*
Margaret Anderson

> *"Love, like fire, can only exist in eternal movement, and love ceases to live as soon as it ceases hoping and fearing."*
>
> La Rochefoucard

SAN DIEGO COAST

Oceanside

Outdoor Kissing

HARBOR BEACH, Oceanside ◆◆◆

Take the Oceanside Harbor exit off Interstate 5 and follow it around to the left. There is a parking lot next to the beach.

About a quarter mile north of the Oceanside Pier lies a tiny stretch of shoreline sandwiched between two jetties called Harbor Beach. Although there is not one particular quality that distinguishes this sunbathing spot from others, it has some features you should know about. First of all, Harbor Beach is fairly quiet. Because it is located at the tweezers' tip of San Diego County, not everyone is willing to travel the distance. Nevertheless, it is well worth the drive. The sand is incredibly white, and a stroll down the rock jetties provides a scenic opportunity for reflection as the waves crash at your feet and surfers glide effortlessly toward you. Also, as its name implies, Harbor Beach rests along the docks, making it a pretty spot from which to watch the boats and the weekend sailors who navigate them. And last but not least, the beach is right next to Cape Cod Village, a small shopping walk reminiscent of an old whaling village, complete with lighthouse. The village has several shops to browse in and some delightful eateries with outdoor patios where you can take in the view. Combine all of these elements and it adds up to a fun and invigorating way to spend a day by the sea.

◆ **Romantic Option:** At the end of Oceanside Pier is **THE FISHERMAN'S RESTAURANT AND BAR**, 1 Oceanside Pier,

Oceanside, (619) 722-2314, (Moderate), where you can study the waters of the Pacific from the upstairs bar or dine leisurely on one of the umbrella-veiled patios. Decorated in nautical style, Fisherman's offers a variety of seafood and pasta dishes. This is a premier spot to people-watch or just feel at one with the sea and each other.

Carlsbad

Hotel/Bed and Breakfast Kissing

PELICAN COVE INN, Carlsbad
320 Walnut Avenue
(619) 434-5995
Moderate to Expensive

Take Interstate 5 to the Carlsbad Village Drive exit. Take Carlsbad Village Drive to Carlsbad Boulevard. Follow Carlsbad Boulevard south to Walnut Avenue. The inn is on the north side of the street.

A cross between a Cape Cod summer home and a gingerbread cottage, this blue-and-pink-trimmed bed and breakfast is sure to delight you. Intricate attention to detail is evident in every room. Enchanting antiques, fluffy featherbed mattresses, wood-burning fireplaces, and beautiful hand-tiled baths are in every suite, two of them with spa tubs. Each of the eight guest chambers also has its own private entry (so you don't have to sneak in late at night) and, best of all, Pelican Cove is just 200 yards from the sparkling blue Pacific—a mere sea breeze away. The owners will be happy to supply you with beach towels, chairs, and picnic baskets during your stay. Mornings at Pelican Cove are greeted with a continental breakfast in the inside dining nook or on the lovely garden patio; in the evening complimentary sherry is served in the lobby.

◆ **Romantic Note:** When you've had enough of the sun, explore Carlsbad, a city said to be reminiscent of early Carmel.

◆   **Romantic Alternative:** We feel some trepidation about recommending **CARLSBAD INN**, 3075 Carlsbad Boulevard, Carlsbad, (619) 434-7020, (800) 235-3939, (Moderate to Expensive), as a romantic alternative. Although it looks lovely—from the outside it resembles a storybook English manor, with cobblestone driveway, cheerful country garden, and climbing ivy—and the view from its well-kept gardens is of the Pacific Ocean below, part of this sizable hotel is a time-share. Every day there's some kind of organized sales activity, such as a barbecue or bingo game, and sales presentations, none of which is the slightest bit tender or affectionate. But if you don't mind all the distractions and hoopla—wow, the ocean-view suites here are spectacular!

Encinitas

Restaurant Kissing

PANNIKIN, Encinitas
510 North Highway 101
(619) 436-5824
Inexpensive to Moderate

Call for directions.

Talk about a great place to wake up and smell the coffee! Though it looks like a cross between a barn and a large country home, this enchanting cafe was once a train station. Now painted a cheery yellow, it's home to an art gallery, a gourmet kitchen shop, and, of course, the Pannikin. Most of the Pannikins have, let's say, interesting decor and this one is no exception. Its loft is eccentrically decorated with a tuba, an abstract nude, and old farm equipment dangling from the high beamed ceiling. One nook even has an enclave of old red vinyl theater-style seats. Enjoy a romantic tete-a-tete under a brightly colored umbrella on the outdoor patio or at a table set up high on the veranda where the towering trees cast their crisp, cooling shadows.

PORTOFINO RESTAURANT, Encinitas
1108 First Street
(619) 942-8442
Moderate to Expensive

From Interstate 5 take the Encinitas Boulevard exit west and turn left at First Street to the restaurant.

Portofino is an exquisite experience for people who like to slowly savor their evening together in an environment conducive to affection and feasting. Though the outside is not enticing, inside you'll understand why this lovely restaurant is booked for special occasions months in advance. Two small dining rooms are located on either side of the main restaurant area, but the most enchanting spot is the enclosed patio that separates them. This brick courtyard is covered with flowers, vine-laced trellises, and wrought-iron tables draped in linen and candlelight. On clear nights, the entire roof rolls back to reveal a sky glittering with stars. Dining out in Encinitas doesn't get much better than this. With such delicious ambience, it's almost asking too much to expect good food, but this is an asset Portofino's is pleased to serve every night. Their fresh abalone (a rarity in these parts), fresh fish, and generous pasta dishes are among the best I've ever had. The tuxedo-clad waiters are doting, friendly, and unpretentious—although they will tempt you into finishing off the evening with a mouth-watering dessert and brandy-kissed cappuccino. It's the Italian way, you know.

◆   **Romantic Alternative:** Every once in a while we uncover an out-of-the-way restaurant that the locals probably wish we hadn't. **LA BONNE BUFFE,** 471 Encinitas Boulevard, Encinitas, (619)436-3081, (Moderate), is a well-kept secret. Tucked in a small shopping center, this lovely French restaurant serves mouth-watering gourmet cuisine in a romantic country setting.

Outdoor Kissing

QUAIL BOTANICAL GARDENS, Encinitas
230 Quail Gardens Drive
(619) 436-3036

From Interstate 5, head east on Encinitas Boulevard one-half mile to Quail Gardens Drive. Turn left into the gardens.

Quail Gardens was donated to the city and taken over by the County Park and Recreation Department more than 30 years ago. It has one of the most diverse plant collections in the world, flaunting more than 5,000 species of exotic trees, palms, ferns, and flowers. You can stroll down its meandering paths for hours , serenaded by singing birds, past lily-covered ponds and surging waterfalls. Resting occasionally on one of the many wooden benches encircled by blossoming greenery, you will feel tranquil and thoroughly romantic.

The park is open seven days a week from 8 A.M. to 5 P.M. Admission is free, but there is a $1 parking fee. Guided tours of the grounds are given at no charge every Saturday at 10 A.M.

Cardiff-by-the-Sea

Hotel/Bed and Breakfast Kissing

CARDIFF-BY-THE-SEA BED AND BREAKFAST
1487 San Elijo
(619) 942-2794
Moderate

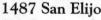 

From the Pacific Coast Highway, head east on Chesterfield and turn right on San Elijo.

This newly opened inn is quickly gaining ground for *one* very special reason: it has only one suite. But (if you'll excuse the pun) how sweet it is! The owners have converted the bottom floor of this seafront summer home into a private bilevel apartment. You can enter through your own door, make cocktails at the wet bar, and curl up with your loved one by a roaring fire and a mesmerizing ocean view. The suite is decorated in white-on-white Spanish tile and comes complete with a wide-screen TV and VCR, an antique pool table, and his-and-hers baths. Picnic baskets, ice chests, and other romantic necessities are also at your disposal. In the morning, you can have breakfast delivered to your room or enjoy it on the sun deck overlooking the sea.

◆ **Romantic Suggestion:** Just down the road is a tiny coffee house with an expansive ocean view. **MIRACLES**, 1955 San Elijo, Cardiff-by-the-Sea, (619) 943-7924, (Inexpensive), offers myriad coffees, baked goods, Italian ices, and healthful sandwiches. It's a laid-back spot to enjoy the sun and the sea, and linger over coffee-flavored kisses.

CARDIFF-BY-THE-SEA LODGE
142 Chesterfield
(619) 944-6474
Moderate to Very Expensive

From Highway 101, go east on Chesterfield. The lodge is about two blocks up on your left.

The Cardiff-by-the-Sea Lodge is a bit of a mixed blessing. Its location overlooking the ocean is fabulous. It's beautifully designed. The rooms are impeccably appointed and rather pretty. But before you start packing your bags and heading for the beach, it's important to note the one and only thing that is lacking: privacy. Most of the rooms are designed to face a walkway or open patio, so unless you have your blinds closed your room is open for public viewing. Also, most of the bathrooms have swinging saloon-style doors instead of floor-to-ceiling doors.

But if you don't mind these issues, you'll consider this lodge a delightful retreat. It is majestically perched on a hill, standing guard over the Cardiff shore. There are 17 enchanting rooms to choose from, depending upon the mood you wish to create. The *Country French Room*

$198.00/night Santa Fe 1st Floor

will warm your hearts with its elegant sitting area, ocean view, and fireplace. The romantic *Southwest Room* includes a four- poster bed swathed in filmy netting, a wet bar, roman tub, panoramic views, and a flagstone hearth. The most expensive room, the *Sweetheart*, is a sight to behold, cloaked in white, with white-water views and a double-sided fireplace that can be enjoyed from both the large heart-shaped whirl-pool tub and the sitting area/bedroom. You may notice that the owner got a little too carried away with hearts here, but it does have the advantage of being the most private and luxurious area in the lodge.

In the morning, the lodge serves an extended continental breakfast that can be eaten in your room, on the flower-filled garden terrace, or on the rooftop, a place popular for weddings and receptions because of its sweeping ocean views.

Restaurant Kissing

CHARLIE'S GRILL, Cardiff-by-the-Sea
2526 South Highway 101
160 **(619) 942-1300**
Moderate

From Interstate 5, take the Lomas Santa Fe exit west, then turn right on Highway 101. The restaurant is about a mile up on your left.

This unassuming seafood restaurant with the unromantic name offers a dining experience brimming with romantic potential. That's because Charlie's is so close to the beach you can practically reach out and touch the frothy waves below. The main dining area downstairs is open and airy, a friendly and casual place where large picture windows frame an indescribably beautiful ocean view. Upstairs is a more formal and elegant retreat paneled in dark woods and decorated in emerald and white. A mirrored wall reflects the sparkling shore. Best of all, as sunlight is replaced by candlelight, you won't have to give up the stunning view, thanks to spotlights that illuminate every crashing wave.

Outdoor Kissing

GLENN PARK, Cardiff-by-the-Sea
Take Highway 101 to Chesterfield East, then take an immediate right on San Elijo. The park will be on your left.

Glenn Park isn't just a pretty place overflowing with shade trees and grassy knolls. It's truly a slice of Southern California life. On the tennis courts bronzed seniors clad in fluorescent pastels engage in lively contests. A few yards away, flat-topped teenagers dart and dash after a basketball. The playground is sprinkled with young parents and their inquisitive toddlers. Though this is not a large park, it has plenty of pretty paths to wander and benches awaiting a lovers' tryst. Better yet, spread out a blanket, curl up together, and just enjoy watching the world go by.

SAN ELIJO STATE BEACH, Cardiff-by-the-Sea
Highway 101 at Chesterfield
(619) 753-5091,(800) 444-7275
Call for directions.

For those adventurous souls who are eager to pitch a tent under the stars, there isn't a better place to do it than San Elijo State Beach, located on a small cliff overlooking the ocean. The prospects here are romantic indeed. By day, you can lounge on the beach below, swim, boogie-board, or scuba dive. By night, you can barbecue in your own private pit, then dine by the glow of moonlight and the sound of the surf.

The sites on the southern end of the campgrounds have the best view of the coastline, especially the La Jolla lights, but the northern sites may be the quietest. The warmer months are always packed, so consider coming here during the fall or late in spring when the sun is still lingering but the tourists are not. The rates range from $14 to $16 a day off-season, and up to $21 for the prime spots at the height of summer. Be sure to make your reservations early.

By the way, you don't have to own an RV or camper to take advantage of this campground. Plenty of romantic sunseekers come by car and slumber in a sleeping bag zipped for two.

◆ **Romantic Warning**: The campgrounds are tucked between the ocean and Old Highway 101, just yards away from the train tracks. While you may find romance in the sound of a locomotive whistle and swear that the clamor of the cars blends in with the sounds of the sea, be forewarned that it can get a bit noisy.

◆ **Romantic Suggestion**: Whether you plan to camp at San Elijo or just drop by for the day, be sure to stop at **SWAMI'S PARK AND LOOKOUT** just a few hundred yards north on Highway 101. Named after the swami who owns the temple adjacent to the park (yes, you are in Southern California), Swami's is more lookout than park, with incredible views of the coastline. Soak up a gorgeous sunset or two.

Del Mar

Hotel/Bed and Breakfast Kissing

L'AUBERGE DEL MAR, Del Mar
1540 Camino del Mar
(619) 259-1515, (800) 553-1336
Expensive to Unbelievably Expensive

At the corner of 15th Street and Camino Del Mar.

Twenty years after the original turn-of-the-century hotel was torn down, L'Auberge Del Mar has gallantly risen from the rubble. Luxuriant, glamorous, and tasteful, the hotel somehow staves off pretentiousness by cultivating a warm French country atmosphere. The lobby, with its enormous fireplace and scattering of overstuffed floral couches and chairs, is oriented toward a wide expanse of french doors that open to admit swift ocean breezes and a majestic view of the glittering coastline below. Fortunately, each of the 123 guest rooms shares in this glory.

And while it would be a dream come true to wake up in L'Auberge's Valentino Suite (named after the famous lover who frequented the original hotel), consider saving your $750 and going down a notch or two to one of the more modest rooms on the third floor, each with vaulted ceiling and fireplace. Of course, wherever you stay here, you're guaranteed a loving escape graced by attentive service and peerless ocean views.

The inn has a first-class spa, tennis courts, private hot-air balloons, and two excellent restaurants. It's also gained quite a reputation for its Sunday brunch and daily afternoon tea.

◆ **Romantic Alternative**: Equally lavish, and almost as intriguing as the The Inn L'Auberge Del Mar, the **INN AT RANCHO SANTE FE**, 5951 Linea Del Cielo, Rancho Santa Fe, (619) 756-1131, (Inexpensive to Expensive), is just seven miles northeast of Del Mar. Nestled in the rolling hills of San Diego's most affluent community, the inn has a congenial, country feeling. It's set on 20 acres of lush greenery, teeming with fragrant eucalyptus trees and sprinkled with more than a dozen small adobe cottages. All of the rooms are individually decorated and many come with a fireplace, wet bar, and private patio. If you tire of lounging, take a swim, play a game or two of tennis, or try your mallet on the inn's championship croquet court. The hotel also has two restaurants; my favorite is the Library, with its book-lined walls and cozy hearth. This inn appeals to a more staid crowd than the Inn at Del Mar, but it still makes a wonderful getaway for anyone looking to relax and take time to smell the well-manicured roses.

THE ROCK HAUS, Del Mar
410 15th Street
(619) 481-3764
Inexpensive to Moderate

Take Camino Del Mar to 15th Street and turn east. The house is half a block up on your left.

This turn-of-the-century mansion, settled into the pine-covered hills of Del Mar, positively oozes romance, with refreshing ocean views at every turn. It's located in the heart of town, a short stroll from the beach and just minutes from the famed Del Mar Racetrack (not a good kissing place).

Though only four of the 10 rooms here have private bathrooms, each has a pleasurable mood all its own. *The Huntsman* is bold and masculine, decorated in tartan and warmed by a wood-burning hearth. The Wicker Garden is more delicate, with peach accents, flowery bed linen, and white wicker furnishings. *The Whale Watch* has a nautical motif, inviting you to scan the seas from the window by day and curl up with *Moby Dick* at night. In the morning a delicious continental breakfast of freshly baked muffins and granola is served on the glass-enclosed sun porch.

Restaurant Kissing

THE BRIGANTINE RESTAURANT, Del Mar
3263 Camino Del Mar
(619) 481-1166
Moderate

Call for directions.

The Brigantine Restaurant looks down at the Del Mar Fairgrounds. A patio table here with a peek of an ocean view could be a pretty romantic place to start off your day before heading to the track. It is also an especially great locale from which to catch a sunset during fair time, as the sunlight gives way to the colorful twinkling of carousels and ferris wheels.

CAFE DEL MAR, Del Mar
1247 Camino Del Mar
(619) 481-1133
Inexpensive to Moderate

At the corner of 13th Street and Highway 101.

Cafe Del Mar is the place to visit when you want to slow down and watch the world go by. Located in the heart of the city, it's decorated in shades of emerald and white, surrounded by huge panels of glass, and has a partially convertible roof. Foliage is everywhere; you'll feel like you're having lunch in a luxurious greenhouse. If you come here during the day, you can watch the quaint community of Del Mar go about its daily business. If you wait until twilight, you can enjoy the cafe's delicious pasta or fresh grilled items by the glint of a star-filled night and draped lights twinkling on the tree-lined perimeter.

IL FORNAIO RESTAURANT, Del Mar
1555 Camino Del Mar
(619) 755-8876
Moderate

From Interstate 5 take Del Mar Heights west to Camino Del Mar and turn right. The Del Mar Plaza will be on your right after you pass 15th Street. Il Fornaio is on the top level.

Imagine that you're dining on the Italian Riviera, basking in an ethereal sunset with the one you love. Too expensive to even fantasize? Gives you more heartburn than heartthrob? Don't worry. Il Fornaio may be the next best thing. Perched on a hill above the sparkling Pacific (you can pretend it's the Mediterranean), this is Del Mar's brightest jewel in the area's treasure chest of restaurants. The interior, a rhapsody of marble and wood, combines Italian tradition and California style. Outside, an attractive glass-enclosed balcony is dotted with umbrellas and star-gazing lovers.

Besides whipping up a breathtaking sunset night after night, Il Fornaio also manages to conjure up all the distinctive tastes and smells of old Italy. From the pasta efieno con gamberetti (spinach and egg linguine sprinkled with shrimp) to the Valentino vestito di nuovo (a three-tiered chocolate masterpiece), the food is like an Italian aria. However, the best news is that the prices are *piu bellisimo*, which translates into "affordable."

◆ **Romantic Note:** Even if Italian food is not your cup of cappuccino, Il Fornaio is worth the trip just to see the view. Drop by the lounge at sunset and enjoy the blissful atmosphere as you watch the sun vanish into the sea.

JAKE'S DEL MAR, Del Mar
1660 Coast Boulevard
(619) 755-2002
Moderate

Take the Via de la Valle west. Turn left at Jimmy Durante Boulevard. At 15th Street take a right, and then another right at Coast Boulevard. Jake's is just past the park on your left.

Sitting at a window table at Jake's is like looking through a kaleidoscope. As the minutes pass, the ocean scene before you is ever-changing. By day, you'll see children frolicking in the surf, sandpipers darting in and out of the waves, and surfers bobbing on the horizon, awaiting the next whitecap. Watch long enough and you'll see families give way to lovers, and the sparkle of the sunlit sea replaced by the sparkle of the stars.

Jake's menu consists of fresh fish, meat, and pasta dishes. Though it's set right on the Del Mar coastline, there is nothing pretentious here. The decor is a simple mix of light woods and lush greenery; the view takes center stage. Jake's has become a very popular place for Sunday brunch, perfect for couples who share a love affair with the sea.

PACIFICA DEL MAR, Del Mar
1555 Camino Del Mar
(619) 792-0476
Moderate

At the corner of 15th Street and Camino Del Mar.

Pacifica Del Mar is romantic Southern California dining just as you would picture it: a warm place to exchange conversation and tender glances against the backdrop of a perfect ocean view. A tanned waitperson rushes to pour your chablis while another arrives with the fresh catch of the day: blackened sea bass served with avocado, cucumber, and tomato salsa. Since its opening, Pacifica Del Mar has quickly gained a reputation for its sensuous seaside locale and delicious California cuisine. The main room is decked in black and white, but softened by ocean-inspired bursts of color. On weekends live jazz trickles throughout the room and onto the romantic glass-enclosed terrace, serenading the setting sun and the special people who have come to bid it adieu.

PANNIKIN, Del Mar
2636 Via de la Valle, Flower Hill Mall
(619) 481-8007
Inexpensive to Moderate

Located in an exclusive shopping center, this is one of the most popular coffeehouses in the area. The reason is its union with the bookstore next door. It's difficult to know where one ends and the other begins, but the marriage between them is perfect. Stocked with art books, classics, and international magazines, **THE BOOK WORKS** is a delightful place to browse before settling in for coffee or a bite to eat next door. On weekends, the place is packed as local area musicians perform live.

SCALINI, Del Mar   ❤ ❤ ❤
3790 Via de la Valle, Suite 301
(619) 259-9944
Moderate

Take Via de la Valle east to El Camino Real. The restaurant is on your left.

Come to Scalini at sunset and you'll have a balcony seat to one of San Diego's most captivating sights. Set just above the polo fields and facing the exclusive estates of Fairbanks Ranch, this also is a great place to watch the early evening parade of hot-air balloons soaring high over Del Mar. But after the balloons settle back down to earth and the colors of sunset give way to night, the restaurant retains a charm all its own, separate from the view. The interior is draped in floral pastels and furnished with dark wood antiques; the outdoor terrace is ideal for a warm-weather rendezvous. The rich Italian fare, featuring great veal dishes, is quite satisfying.

TARYN'S AT THE TRACK, Del Mar
514 Via de la Valle
(619) 481-8300
Inexpensive to Moderate

From Interstate 5, head west on Via de la Valle. Look carefully for the sign about two blocks up on the right.

Recently, a local television station called Taryn's San Diego's most romantic restaurant. Having spent a fair amount of my career in a TV newsroom, I was instantly dubious. Newspeople are not exactly romantic; they tend to be skeptical and jaded. In Taryn's case, the media folks were right on. The fetching Southwestern decor has all the colors of a Del Mar sunset. The intimate gray leather booths, blushing with salmon-colored tablecloths and trimmed in pastel Aztec prints, were set far enough apart for intimate repartee. Candlelight flickered through cutouts in the adobe wall that partitioned the dining area, casting mysterious shadows across the room. The restaurant serves wonderful pasta, meat, and seafood dishes, and offers a luscious macadamia nut cheesecake.

◆ **Romantic Warning**: Getting a table here during racing season is not worth the wait or the crowds. Your amorous mood will be better served when the horses and jockeys have the day off.

Outdoor Kissing

SEA GROVE PARK, Del Mar

At the corner of 15th Street and Coast Boulevard.

Every once in a while it is difficult to reveal a place you'd rather keep to yourself. What a dilemma. But if you promise to keep this just between us, we'll share this one with you.

If you wander down 15th Street in Del Mar, you'll come across a tiny patch of paradise known as Sea Grove Park. Poised above the ocean, this is an ideal spot in which to curl up with your beau, a bottle of wine, and a fresh, crusty loaf of bread. Mother Nature conducts a symphony of colors here nightly as the sun goes down and the surfers wait for their next ride in to shore.

SKYSURFER, Del Mar
1221 Camino Del Mar
(619) 481-6800
Very Expensive

Several hot-air balloon companies are based in and near the Del Mar area. This one has a very good reputation, but there are others. Check the phone book for names and phone numbers.

Almost every evening of the year, the skies above Del Mar burst with brilliant color. One of the most romantic ways to view this awesome display is from the basket of a hot-air balloon. The feel of the wind caressing your skin and the taste of the salt air at these heights are ethereal. As the massive balloon fills with hot air and you float upward, the sea below takes center stage costumed by the sunset. At the end of your evening flight you'll be given champagne and truffles to complete the fantasy. Sure, it's expensive and frivolous, but your heightened feelings afterward will be priceless.

La Jolla

La Jolla translated from Spanish means "the jewel," and such a name is no exaggeration for this town. Its rugged coastline is splashed with white sand beaches and foamy azure waves. The downtown is replete with art galleries, posh boutiques, and fine restaurants. The rolling hillsides are dotted with palatial mansions and winding roads. Some people consider La Jolla a bit garish, others think that it's merely extravagant. *It is* thoroughly Californian, in its own way romantic and worth visiting. And there is enough kissing territory to keep you busy from dawn to dusk: checking out Windansea Beach, hiking through Torrey Pines State Reserve, and strolling along the grassy knolls above the beach are just a few options. The beauty of this gem of a town is in the eyes of the beholder.

Hotel/Bed and Breakfast Kissing

BED AND BREAKFAST INN AT LA JOLLA, La Jolla ❤❤❤
7753 Draper Avenue
(619) 456-2066
Inexpensive to Very Expensive

Take Prospect south to Draper and turn left. The inn is located across the street from the Museum of Contemporary Art.

No other bed and breakfast in La Jolla has the polished warmth of this inn. It's easy to see how it became a source of inspiration for composer John Philip Sousa, who lived here during the '20s. You will want to make your own music in one of its 16 inviting rooms—perhaps the white-on-white *Holiday Suite* with its four-poster bed and large inviting fireplace. Or the *Pacific View*, decorated in nautical style, where you can enjoy the most arresting seascape in the house. Each room has a different theme, from Victorian to Latin to Oriental, and all have private baths. Fresh fruit and sherry await your arrival.

A light breakfast is served in the inn's quaint but elegant dining room. It's never too early to sip mimosas from Waterford crystal or pull out the good silver for a cup of coffee or tea. Wine and cheese are offered from 4 P.M. to 6 P.M. With a day's notice, the innkeeper will be happy to pack you a picnic lunch for an amorous afternoon at the beach.

◆ **Romantic Alternative: SCRIPP'S INN**, 555 Coast Boulevard, La Jolla, (619) 454-3391, (Moderate to Expensive), barely squeaks into the Bed and Breakfast category. Sure, this remodeled 1942 lodge serves a continental breakfast, but you have to come down to the tiny lobby, pile a tray full of croissant, muffins, coffee, and juice, and take it back to your room. Why include it then? Although its inside is nothing special, the inn resides on a premier piece of oceanfront property. The accommodations are indeed cozy and two of the units have a fireplace and private terrace. The fireplace rooms are the ones we recommend. They have the best seaside vistas and the most privacy.

LA VALENCIA HOTEL, La Jolla
1132 Prospect Street
(619) 454-0771
Expensive to Unbelievably Expensive

On Prospect Street near Herschel.

Regal La Valencia is a pastel pink hotel that blends serenely with the famous rose-colored sunsets of La Jolla. The hotel was built in the '20s, and because it claimed the most stunning stretch of shoreline in the city it soon became a star-studded landmark. Its glamour and opulence still flourish today. There are 100 lavish guest rooms and suites to choose from, all decorated in classic European style. You can enjoy the shimmering view from your room or curl up in the cozy lobby area as you listen to a pianist serenade the setting sun.

La Valencia has three restaurants, but it's the **SKY ROOM,** on the top floor of the hotel, that will make a lasting impression on you. See the separate listing in the La Jolla Restaurant Kissing section for more details.

Restaurant Kissing

BERNINI'S, La Jolla
7550 Fay Avenue
(619) 454-5013
Inexpensive

Call for directions.

Bernini's is off the beaten track on a La Jolla side street, but it certainly didn't take long for people to find out about it. The outside awning reads "Espresso, Gelato, and Magazini", and that's exactly what you'll find here; gourmet coffees, delicious gelato, tantalizing baked goods, and an extensive variety of international magazines available for purchase. As you'd expect, the crowd here is also quite international, which only adds to the romantic intrigue.

BRAVO! BARCELONA, La Jolla
1295 Prospect Street, Suite 201
(619) 456-1579
Moderate

Take Torrey Pines Road to Prospect and turn left.

Bravo! Barcelona is romantic in a way unlike any other restaurant. Although it has a dazzling view of the La Jolla Cove, soft Spanish music, and even candlelight, that's where the semblance stops. The walls here are full of bright colors and abstract art. The mood is festive and the service, well, a little zany. After a while, you begin to feel like dancing on the table with a rose between your teeth. Go figure.

Maybe it's just the enthusiasm with which your every need is indulged. Or perhaps it's the zesty *tapas* (appetizers) that tempt your taste buds and rouse your appetite for more. Then again, it could be that everyone is having a good time because it's just so much fun to eat here. After all, where else would you find the chef being introduced for his nightly standing ovation or the waiters yelling *"Ole!"* to salute a broken dish?

Don't get me wrong. If you want to be left alone to gaze at the view and raise a toast to the stars, your discreet waiter will see to that. But if you'd like to find an enjoyable alternative to pre-packaged romance, say *"Si"* to Bravo! Barcelona.

CAFE 928, La Jolla
928 Silverado Street
(619) 454-8977
Inexpensive to Moderate

Call for directions

This tiny brick cottage welcomes its customers with the enticing aromas of freshly brewed gourmet coffees and tantalizing sweets. While the cafe is quite casual, its decor hints of a subtle elegance. Sit inside or join the sun worshipers and people watchers out on its diminutive front patio.

THE COTTAGE RESTAURANT, La Jolla
7702 Fay Avenue
(619) 454-8409
Inexpensive

On the corner of Fay and Kline.

This beachside bungalow is brimming with romance. A white picket fence, lots of colorful flowers, and a sea of pastel and floral umbrellas shading the brick patio seating area spotlight the outside. Inside, pastel watercolors of the La Jolla shore accentuate the cheerful motif. Hot coffee and waffles smothered with bananas and strawberries complete an enchanting La Jolla dining experience just too good to miss.

ELARIO'S RESTAURANT, La Jolla
7955 La Jolla Shores Drive
(619) 459-0541
Moderate to Expensive

From Interstate 5 South: Take the La Jolla Village Drive turnoff and head west. Turn left onto Torrey Pines Road and you'll see the Summerhouse Inn on your right as the road merges into Ardath. Elario's Restaurant is located on top of the Summerhouse Inn. From Interstate 5 North: Take the Ardath turnoff and turn right onto La Jolla Shores Drive.

The soft music, the candlelight, and the views of La Jolla's shoreline are so heavenly that angels would feel right at home at Elario's, an elegant restaurant perched atop the Summerhouse Inn, one of the few high-rises in the city. The hotel itself is OK but not worth listing. The main attraction is the penthouse restaurant, which attracts aroused appetites from all over the world. The best seats in the house are the row of intimate banquettes that line the floor-to-ceiling windows. Here, side-by-side, you and your special someone can feast on both the view and the restaurant's gourmet cuisine. The extensive wine cellar has more than 1,000 labels from which to choose. Elario's also has a delectable champagne brunch served Sundays between 10 A.M. and 2 P.M.

◆   **Romantic Option:** If chateaubriand and white-glove service is a bit stuffy for your taste, you'll still find romance at Elario's. The lounge features some of the best jazz in all of San Diego, with moonglow on the ocean as a backdrop. Because of its popularity the room may be crowded, but persistent couples can always find a spot on the dance floor for a little cheek-to-cheek.

FRENCH GOURMET, La Jolla
711 Pearl Street
(619) 454-6736
Inexpensive

Near the corner of Pearl and Draper.

You know those coffee commercials where people sip their morning brew and are instantly transported to a sidewalk cafe in Paris? Like magic, they can smell the French bread baking and hear the language of love echoing through the streets. That's what a trip to French Gourmet is like.

This very small, very simple restaurant has no tablecloths, no crystal chandeliers. It is the kind of bistro you'd likely discover in the rural neighborhoods of France, with six booths divided by lace curtains and ten tiny tables squeezed side by side. For intimacy's sake a booth is preferable, but there is also something exciting about sitting in the midst of so many duos caught up in profound discussion, candlelight dancing on their faces. The extraordinary cuisine, the mouth-watering desserts, and the authentic European ambience will lure you back for more.

GEORGE'S AT THE COVE, La Jolla
1250 Prospect Street
(619) 454-4244
Inexpensive to Expensive

Call for directions.

George's at the Cove is yet another oceanfront restaurant with a dazzling view. But what makes this place special is the fact that it is divided into three separate dining areas that cater individually to your taste and budget. The main dining room maintains a congenial elegance. More laid back are **GEORGE'S CAFE AND BAR** and its new **OCEAN TERRACE**. Both serve a menu of lighter, less expensive entrees enhanced by ocean breezes and spectacular coastline views.

IL COVO COFFEEHOUSE, La Jolla
1255 Coast Boulevard
(619) 459-3675
Inexpensive

Take Torrey Pines Road to Prospect and veer right onto Coast Boulevard. Il Covo will be on your left.

Though Il Covo's interior is tiny, the view of the La Jolla coastline is immense. In the mornings, drowsy-eyed lovers flock here to start their day with a strong espresso and a freshly baked muffin or two. Evenings, they converge to watch the sunset, thumb through a magazine purchased from Il Covo's small news rack, and go over the events of the day. The crowds are often artsy and decidedly eclectic: young and old, conservative and not so conservative. The decor lends itself to such eccentricity: the colors are muted, the mirrors are gilded, and they change the paintings on the walls monthly.

◆ **Romantic Warning:** Because Il Covo has such an ideal location, it has become quite popular. The coffeehouse is extremely small, so it fills up quickly. To avoid the crowds, come on weekdays or weekend nights.

L'AUBERGE, La Jolla
1237 Prospect Street
(619) 454-2524
Inexpensive

In the "International Shops" walkway on Prospect Street.

After hearing promising things about L'Auberge we couldn't wait to see if our information was correct. It sounded too good to be true. But true it is. Who could resist such tempting trappings? L'Auberge is a beautiful, intimate confection whipped up in shades of blush and mint. The air dances with the sounds of French music and the smells of mouth-watering gourmet cuisine. Every detail seems to cater to matters of *amour*.

MARINE ROOM, La Jolla
2000 Spindrift Drive
(619) 459-7222
Moderate to Expensive

Take the Ardath exit off Interstate 5. The Marine Room is in the Spindrift Hotel, about a mile up the road on your right.

Separated from the sea by only a narrow stretch of sand, this steak-and-seafood restaurant is as close as you can get to the ocean without getting your feet wet. In fact, during high tide don't be surprised to find frothy waves lapping at the windows. In the 50 years it's been in business, the Marine Room has been washed out twice during violent storms. Each time it was lovingly restored and its one-inch-thick glass panes reinstalled. It's this tenacity that has drawn couples, generation after generation, to the Marine Room's premier corner tables. Unlike many seaside restaurants, which look out onto a black void after sunset, the Marine Room illuminates its stretch of beach so you're never without a mesmerizing ocean view.

MILLIGAN'S, La Jolla
5786 La Jolla Boulevard
(619) 459-7311
Inexpensive

One block north of Bird Rock Avenue, on La Jolla Boulevard.

Romance is in the eye (or the heart) of the beholder. What delights one couple may indeed disappoint another. Some like their restaurants casual, others desire a more elegant atmosphere. Milligan's is the perfect answer for either taste. The main floor feels formal. The dark wood paneling encases rich leather booths that are partitioned by etched glass panels. Mirrored ceilings, illuminated by art deco sconces, reflect the images of people in love. Request a table upstairs and you'll discover a lighter, more casual atmosphere, plus an ocean view that will take your breath away. Everything here is bright and festive: the walls and tablecloths are white, but colorful accents spring from the modern mural that borders the ceiling.

The menu is absolutely American. Milligan's is famous for their country-fried steak, but you can also get your fillet smothered with bearnaise sauce. Milligan's also offers an enticing Sunday brunch, complimentary sunset hors d'oeuvres in the upstairs bar, and a nightly piano bar on the main floor where you can sip and swoon.

PANNIKIN, La Jolla
7467 Girard Avenue
(619) 454-5453
Inexpensive to Moderate

Call for directions

OK, let's give credit where credit is due. Long before coffee bars were the rage, the Pannikin in La Jolla was brewing. For years it's been the hangout of couples looking for a pleasant place to share a cappuccino and some intimate conversation. Our favorite spot is the corner table on Pannikin's front terrace, sheltered by an enormous shade tree and cooled by sea-kissed breezes.

SANTE RISTORANTE, La Jolla
7811 Herschel Avenue
(619) 454-1315
Moderate

The restaurant is two blocks east of Prospect on Herschel.

Though this restaurant is charming by day, it becomes even more special at night when the oak-shaded terrace is illuminated by twinkling lights that mingle gently with the evening stars. And while most couples prefer to sit in the flower-covered brick courtyard, the dining room is also desirable, minus the balmy breeze and fresh air. The decor, in subtle shades of gray and beige, combines modern chic with bits of old Italy. This tasteful interior is matched by a menu that wins over critics and patrons alike. The chef uses nothing but the finest ingredients, many flown here from Europe on a daily basis. It all adds up to an outstanding meal in a very romantic context.

◆   **Romantic Alternative**: Simple decor in emerald and white is what you'll find at **THE UPSTAIRS CAFE**, 8008 Girard Avenue, La Jolla, (619) 454-8884, (Moderate). (No need to overdecorate a restaurant that is situated atop an exciting stretch of shoreline in La Jolla.) But perhaps the best thing about this California bistro is that you don't have to be dressed up to enjoy it. Instead, you can join the eclectic mix of sun worshipers and business folk, La Jollans and international jet-setters, who have been attracted by the good French cuisine, a laudable wine list, and the setting sun.

THE SKY ROOM, La Jolla   ◆◆◆◆
1132 Prospect Street, in the La Valencia Hotel
(619) 454-0771
Very Expensive

On Prospect Street near Herschel.

So you say you want the very best. You're ready for a romantic, elegant, money-is-no-object evening. Where can you go to celebrate that all-important occasion? The Sky Room at La Valencia should be at the top of your list. It's a tiny room with an enormously beautiful ocean view and only ten small tables to share it. Each is bathed in candlelight and set with the finest silver and Wedgwood china. Awash in shades of mauve, this lovely French restaurant is constantly embellished by the sky's ever-changing color palette. Having dinner at the Sky Room is truly like being on a cloud.

TOP O' THE COVE RESTAURANT, La Jolla
1216 Prospect Street
(619) 454-7779
Expensive

Take Torrey Pines Road south to Prospect Street and turn right to the restaurant.

If table 6 could talk, you would hear stories of eternal devotion and passionate proposals whispered between savory courses. Table 6 is the spot every romantic couple asks for (we had to beg) when dining at Top o' the Cove. In fact, it's often booked weeks in advance. In this elegant gingerbread cottage on the sea, table 6 is like a balcony seat over La Jolla's shimmering shoreline, set in a tiny, private alcove. Through an open window you can feel the sea breeze on your face. Of course, almost every table in Top o' the Cove is a ticket to an unforgettable meal. Though the double waiter service is a bit pretentious and overeager, the atmosphere and gourmet cuisine are excellent.

◆   **Romantic Note:** Top O' the Cove has added on a new bistro terrace where you can sip cocktails at sunset and dine on light cuisine that's easy on your wallet. I'll toast to that!

Outdoor Kissing

LA JOLLA COVE

Heading south on Torrey Pines Road, turn right onto Prospect. Stay to the right and take Coast Boulevard down to the beach.

Walking along the sandy shores of La Jolla Cove, you can understand why this area's been likened to the French Riviera. Although there are miles of brilliant beaches throughout Southern California, the water here seems bluer somehow, the sand a bit whiter, and the sunsets more spectacular. Linger over a picnic lunch on the expansive lawn area, **ELLEN SCRIPPS BROWNING PARK**, or dive right into the aquamarine waves. The cove is a perfect place to snorkel or skin-dive, with an abundance of fascinating reefs, caves, and tide pools to explore. And if you're in the mood for a refreshing dip, this one-mile stretch of beach, protected from ocean swells, is great swimming territory. Afterward, find your own private place in the sun on one of the many cliffs overlooking the cove. The view from these vantage points is unrivaled.

TORREY PINES STATE RESERVE, La Jolla
(619) 755-2063

From Interstate 5, take the Carmel Valley Road exit and go west to Camino Del Mar. Turn left; the entrance to the park will be on your right.

This state reserve spans 2,000 acres of San Diego's most majestic shoreline and is home to the rarest pine trees in the nation. In addition, more than 300 other plants and flowers grow wild here, perfuming the air with a bouquet of fragrances. You can spend the day basking in the sun on the reserve's flawless length of beach or hiking along one of its five winding trails to find jutting cliffs, windswept canyons, and wondrous ocean views.

Perhaps the reserve's most beautiful path is the **GUY FLEMING TRAIL**, which fortunately is also its easiest. Six-tenths of a mile long, it meanders past etched sandstone formations and includes some of the park's most stupendous vistas. Torrey Pines is the perfect spot to commune with nature and each other.

◆ **Romantic Note:** Because this is a state reserve, there is great concern over maintaining the ecological balance. That means no smoking, picnicking, or collecting of flowers or pine cones anywhere in the reserve. There are, however, some picnic benches along the beach. Both areas are free to visitors who come on foot or bicycle; it costs $4 on weekends to park your car.

WINDANSEA BEACH, La Jolla

Take Coast Boulevard to Nautilus Street, turn west and drive until you reach Windansea Beach.

This beach is right out of the love scene in *From Here to Eternity*. Don't be surprised if you get an irresistible urge to grab your loved one and run along the sand hand-in-hand, only to fall into its surf in a passionate embrace. Made famous by the Beach Boys in the '60s, Windansea is caressed by large waves and lined with rocky ridges. Open up a picnic basket on the shore or on the grassy bluffs above the beach. If you're really lucky, you can claim the thatched cabana that has sheltered lovers from the sun for as long as anyone can remember.

Pacific Beach

Restaurant Kissing

EL CHALAN RESTAURANT, Pacific Beach
1050 Garnet Street
(619) 459-7707
Moderate

Take the Grand/Garnet turnoff from Interstate 5 and follow Garnet to the restaurant.

On weekends young people from all over San Diego scramble to Pacific Beach in search of nightlife. Its streets are engulfed by cars from which loud music blares. Caught in the midst of the madness, but worlds away from it in atmosphere, is El Chalan Restaurant.

There is something soothing about this elegant dining establishment. Perhaps it's the tables draped in pink and sparkling with candlelight, and the way the light reflects from the mirrored walls and crystal chandeliers. This is an ideal setting in which to enjoy steak and seafood dishes enhanced by creamy sauces and heartwarming conversation. The outdoor patio is also quite romantic, especially when the roving guitarist serenades you under pale moonlight.

FIREHOUSE BEACH CAFE, Pacific Beach
722 Grand Avenue
(619) 272-1999
Inexpensive to Moderate

Right next to the fire station at the corner of Grand Avenue and Mission Boulevard.

Breakfast can be a thoroughly romantic meal, particularly when you are gazing at one another over steaming coffee and buttermilk pancakes or strawberry french toast—like the kind they make at the Firehouse Beach Cafe. Besides hearty breakfast treats, they also dish up a lively ocean view here. The wood-shingled sun deck overlooks the Pacific Beach boardwalk and is within earshot of the crashing waves below. The prices are more than reasonable, and everything about the place is pleasant and casual.

LAMONT STREET GRILL, Pacific Beach
4445 Lamont Street
(619) 270-3060
Inexpensive to Moderate

Take the Grand Street turnoff from Interstate 5 and head south. Turn right at Lamont.

Do you love dining near the beach but find that all too often the best restaurants have restrictive dress codes and high-tone atmospheres? The Lamont Street Grill is an energizing alternative. This affable beach bungalow combines refinement with welcoming, casual, California style. You can dine on the patio illuminated by a glowing fireplace and a spreading oak tree strung with white flickering lights, or sit in one of the small pastel dining rooms bathed in candlelight. There are plenty of private nooks and crannies and corner tables to choose from and lots of gourmet items to stimulate your taste buds. When you've finished dinner, the chocolate-dipped fresh fruit is on the house.

ZANZIBAR COFFEEHOUSE, Pacific Beach
976 Garnet Avenue
(619) 272-4762
Inexpensive

From Interstate 5 take the Grand/Garnet turnoff and head west on Garnet.

To call Zanzibar eclectic doesn't do it justice. Just blocks from the beach, this coffeehouse has been a raving success with people watchers who like great coffee and a variety of baked goods, desserts, quiches, and sandwiches. The decor is as diverse as the people who enter. The beige walls are lined with large, abstruse paintings, and each tabletop is different in size, texture or color. The music you sip by may be '30s blues or '90s rock, depending upon the tastes of the people who serve you.

Outdoor Kissing

FANUEL STREET PARK, Pacific Beach
4000 block of Fanuel

Take the Grand/Garnet exit off Interstate 5 and follow Grand west to Ingraham. Turn left on Fanuel; the park is at the end of the road.

Fanuel Park is a special place for a special kind of lovers: parents. Just because you've had kids doesn't mean you can't or shouldn't make time to enjoy the romantic side of life.

This bayside jewel is just one shining example of the kind of daytime outing that will please everyone in the family. There's an expansive playground, a nice lawn for picnicking, and a striking view of the Riviera Shores. It's an ideal spot to sunbathe or to rollerblade, stroll, or bicycle along the path that winds around the cove. Anyone can appreciate the beauty of Fanuel Park, but for romance-hungry parents it's a dream come true.

◆   **Romantic Alternatives:** Other scenic spots with swing sets in the greater San Diego area include **GLORIETTA BAY PARK** (a half mile southeast of the Hotel Del Coronado on Orange Street), **POWERHOUSE PARK** (north of 15th Street on Coast Boulevard), and **TIDELANDS PARK** (located at the base of the Coronado Bridge).

KATE SESSIONS PARK, Pacific Beach

From the Pacific Beach area of San Diego, take Grand Avenue west from Interstate 5 and turn right on Lamont. Kate Sessions is on your right as you head up the hill.

If you've ever wondered what it's like to peer down on San Diego from on high, take a trip to Kate Sessions Park, which overlooks some of the city's most astounding scenery. The unencumbered panoramic view stretches from the ocean to the mountains, across to Coronado and beyond. Bring a picnic basket and someone you love: there's nothing like snuggling on a blanket as the water sparkles below, the birds serenade from the trees, and the clouds slowly drift by.

◆ **Romantic Consideration:** No reason to end your romantic adventures here. After you've spent the afternoon at Kate Sessions, watch the sunset from **MOUNT SOLEDAD.** This is a somewhat notorious spot for parking, but unfortunately there's not much space for anything else. Nevertheless, it's worth the trip to see this beautiful bird's-eye view of La Jolla and the San Diego area.

Mission Beach and Mission Bay

Restaurant Kissing

INVADER CRUISES, Mission Bay
1066 North Harbor Drive
(619) 234-8687, (800) 262-4386
Moderate to Expensive

Call for directions

Imagine gliding along the water at night with the city lights reflecting on the water's glassy, calm surface, forming colorful beams that ripple at the slightest movement. That's what awaits you aboard an Invader Dinner Cruise. As sunlight is replaced by starlight, you'll dine, dance, and share some quiet moments alone on deck. OK, so maybe some of the other passengers had the same sneaky idea, but with such a breathtaking, 360-degree view of the downtown harbor, who could resist a moonlit kiss?

Outdoor Kissing

BELMONT PARK, Mission Beach

On the beach at Mission Boulevard and West Mission Bay Drive.

We were thrilled when they saved Belmont Park. Its 1925 roller coaster is not only a historical monument, but a friendly reminder that maybe we all take life a little too seriously. Perhaps it's time to let our hair down.

Now completely restored, *The Giant Dipper* is finally back on track. It's accompanied by a beautiful new shopping complex that offers a myriad of captivating diversions, such as ocean-view restaurants, gift and specialty stores, and a delightful merry-go-round. If you're ready to tackle the roller coaster, just follow the familiar screams to the line of couples waiting to climb aboard, and remember to hold on tight!

Belmont Park also lays claim to the largest indoor swimming pool this side of the Mississippi, *The Plunge*. While this may not seem too alluring, they offer *dive-in movies* during the summer, where you provide the inner tube and they provide the classic films.

MISSION BAY PARK

Call or stop by the Visitor Information Center, located at the corner of East Mission Bay Drive and Clairemont Drive, (619) 276-8200, for detailed information on Mission Bay recreational equipment rentals.

It isn't uncommon for San Diegans to look up or down the coast to find romantic things to do. Everyone needs to get away and escape their day-to-day surroundings. But what about the beauty that lies in their own backyard? Maybe it's time to took a second look. Start with Mission Bay Park.

When was the last time you rented a jet ski, sailed a catamaran across the sun-sequined water, or cycled the length of Sail Bay? How about a picnic at Crown Point, a bonfire on Fiesta Island, or some kite flying at Tecolate Shores? The possibilities are endless. This enormous marine park spans more than 4,600 acres, offering 27 miles of shoreline, 19 of which are sandy beaches. By day or by night, Mission Bay offers fun and romance served on a sparkling aquamarine platter. Go on, indulge yourselves.

Ocean Beach

Hotel/Bed and Breakfast Kissing

THE ELSBREE HOUSE, Ocean Beach
5054 Narragansett Avenue
(619) 226-4133
Inexpensive

Follow Sunset Cliffs Boulevard to Narragansett Avenue and go west.

Ocean Beach is known more for its radical eccentricity than its passion potential. The exception to that reputation is this adorable Cape Cod bed and breakfast less than a block from the beach and within walking distance of the heart of this funky seaside town. Beyond the french doors, you'll find guest rooms that are both designer-perfect and warmly inviting. White wicker furniture tucked in shady nooks on the terrace and a small garden patio provide the perfect backdrop for a relaxing afternoon. Best of all, at these prices you'll still have money left over to buy a romantic dinner for two, treat yourselves to a moonlit cruise, or splurge on an extravagant bottle of wine to be enjoyed in your private quarters. What's more, the innkeeper is a romantic at heart and will be more than happy to head you in the direction of the most intimate cafes, restaurants, and beaches in the area. This is budget kissing at its finest.

◆ **Romantic Alternative:** Just a few blocks away, you'll find **QUIGG'S**, 5083 Santa Monica Avenue, Ocean beach, (619) 222-1101, (Inexpensive to Moderate). In contrast to the more formal-feeling Ocean Beach restaurants, Quigg's offers a very casual ambience garnished by a captivating ocean view. Set across from the Ocean Beach Pier, the booths are cozy, the service is friendly, and the steak, seafood, and pasta dishes are tempting. Be sure to make your reservations early enough to catch the sunset.

Restaurant Kissing

THEE BUNGALOW, Ocean Beach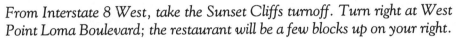
4996 West Point Loma Boulevard
(619) 224-2884
Moderate

From Interstate 8 West, take the Sunset Cliffs turnoff. Turn right at West Point Loma Boulevard; the restaurant will be a few blocks up on your right.

Visiting Thee Bungalow is like taking a trip to the house of an old friend, one who has excellent taste in wine and art and who lovingly serves guests his gourmet cuisine. Each room in this beach-cottage-turned-restaurant has appeal, but the living room area is most aglow with romance. Here, under a lofty wood-beamed ceiling, couples dine by candlelight and the amber glow of a blazing fire. Lace curtains, mahogany shutters, and spotlighted oil paintings all lend a feeling of country elegance. Thee Bungalow offers steak, chicken, and salmon, but the real specialty is roast duckling. Only in Ocean Beach would you find discount duck night, when you can dine on Donald for a paltry (or poultry) $8.95 Tuesday through Thursday and Sunday. Sunday brunch here is impressive, with interesting items such as a Brie omelet and duck machaca.

◆ **Romantic Alternative: THE BELGIAN LION**, 2265 Bacon Street, Ocean Beach, (619) 223-2700, (Moderate to Expensive), just across the street from Thee Bungalow, has a very different romantic style. This provincial restaurant is set off by crisp white tablecloths and Belgian lace curtains with a delicate tapestry trim. The shelves proudly display copper cookware, and the walls are hung with works by Flemish masters. Add to this doting service and rich French cuisine (steak, fresh fish, rabbit) and you have an evening made for two.

Outdoor Kissing

SUNSET CLIFFS, Ocean Beach

Take the Sunset Cliffs Boulevard exit off Interstate 8 and follow it around until you reach the cliffs.

The winding road that leads to the cliffs is embraced by the sea on one side, lined by spectacular homes on the other. Because it's a residential area, there are no signs to mar the view, no tall buildings to obstruct its sunsets, and no swarms of people to compete for its viewing space. On almost any day you'll find only a few cars pulled over to drink in the view, while a handful of adventurers scale down its cliffs to a sandy spot perfect for capturing the sun's vivid exit at the day's end. With nothing but sparkling water on all sides, you will feel as though you're sitting on the edge of the world. In amazement you will watch as the sky explodes into brilliant color, painting a giant golden brushstroke across the ice blue ocean. You will swear that you can hear a sizzle as the sun melts into the sea.

Harbor Island and Shelter Island

Hotel/Bed and Breakfast Kissing

BOAT AND BREAKFAST, Harbor Island
and Shelter Island
(619) 223-3477
Expensive to Unbelievably Expensive

Call for directions.

Those who have had enough of Victorian bed and breakfasts with lacy accents and stuffed teddies in wicker rockers will love this entry. Boat and Breakfast provides a nautical escape, where you can spend the night on a yacht and be rocked to sleep by the tide. For little more than the price of a hotel room, your stay can include sunbathing on the deck, cooking dinner on board, and dining on the fantail. The yachts range from beautifully appointed sailing boats to magnificent ocean-going vessels, and include TV, stereo, CD player, microwave, and refrigerator. And while the boats are intended to remain dockside, for a hefty $100 to $200 an hour it's possible to hire a crew for a trip on the local high seas. Regardless, come morning, a light breakfast is served aboard.

Coronado

Take Interstate 5 to the Coronado Toll Bridge. Or take Highway 5 south past San Diego to Palm Avenue. Turn west and take Silver Strand Boulevard to Coronado.

Some places seem more like film sets than like anything real, places that are just too beautiful to be true. Like Coronado, for instance. To begin with, the two primary ways to get there are via the Coronado Bridge, which soars high above the downtown skyline, or on a ferryboat cruise across the silvery bay. Once you arrive, the palm-tree-lined streets, the winding bike trails, the manicured neighborhoods, the sandy beaches, and the sweeping vistas will keep you occupied for hours, if not days. This perfect little peninsula is San Diego's own personal Oz, and a great place for fun, sightseeing, and most definitely for romancing.

◆ **Romantic Note:** For ferry information to Coronado, see the Coronado Ferry entry in the Outdoor Kissing section of the San Diego.

Hotel/Bed and Breakfast Kissing

HOTEL DEL CORONADO, Coronado
1500 Orange Avenue
(619) 522-8000
Expensive to Unbelievably Expensive

From the Coronado Bridge, take Fourth Avenue to Orange. Turn left and follow the road for about two miles to the hotel.

The century-old Hotel Del Coronado is a place of legendary liaisons and romances. Case in point: in 1920, the Prince of Wales met the woman of his dreams during a visit here. He later abdicated his throne as the King of England to marry the former Coronado housewife and the two became known as the Duke and Duchess of Windsor.

From its towering turrets to the artistically carved wood interior, *The Del* (as it is known by locals) is thoroughly beguiling. Little about the original structure has changed since Thomas Edison pulled the switch on the hotel's first lighted Christmas tree. Marilyn Monroe filmed *Some Like It Hot* on its golden beaches; President Nixon hosted a lavish state dinner here. However, the hotel has added two ocean towers and spruced up most of its 700 rooms and suites, fortunately without disturbing much of the original ambience for which this Victorian hotel is so famous.

When it comes to romance, a big hotel usually isn't better. Yet a stay at this sizable resort promises plenty of tempting distractions and leisurely activities. The Del has two swimming pools; three restaurants (the Crown Room Restaurant has just undergone a million-dollar restoration), one with a view of the water; tennis courts; dozens of shops; and a world-famous health spa. But best of all, it is nestled between the sparkling Pacific and Glorietta Bay, leaving lots of open spaces for wandering, picnicking, and sunbathing.

◆ **Romantic Alternative:** If the Hotel Del Coronado is booked, take a peek at **LE MERIDIAN**, 2000 Second Street, Coronado, (619) 435-3000, (Expensive to Very Expensive). This waterfront resort sits at the foot of the Coronado Bridge and claims a glorious view of the bay and downtown skyline. Every one of its 300 rooms is decorated in French country patterns and embellished with a lovely view from a private terrace. The hotel has two restaurants, a European spa, tennis courts, and just about anything else you could possibly want or need. If Le Meridian is out of your price range, you could still stop by for lunch or dinner at **L'ESCALE**, their terrace restaurant. The view is stupendous and the prices are very reasonable.

◆ **Second Romantic Alternative: GLORIETTA BAY INN**, 1630 Glorietta Boulevard, Coronado, (619) 435-3101, (800) 283-9383,

(Inexpensive to Unbelievably Expensive), is across the street from Hotel Del Coronado. This stunning white mansion, once owned by John Spreckels, now holds a bewildering jumble of beautifully renovated rooms that face Glorietta Bay and an assortment of more motel-like accommodations. The guest rooms in the main house are the most desirable and proved to be our favorites. They are also the most expensive, but something this special is worth it.

LOEWS, Coronado   ◆◆
4000 Coronado Bay Road
(619)424-4000, (800) 23-LOEWS
Very Expensive to Unbelievably Expensive

Call for directions.

You could say that Loews is the newest kid on the luxury resort block in this very exclusive neighborhood. South of Hotel Del Coronado and directly across Silver Strand Beach, Loews is indeed a premier port of call. The resort occupies its own private peninsula and offers incredible views of the bay. The rooms are also beautiful, especially the lavish seaside villas (a mere $375 a night), but despite its many amenities, the hotel is still large and impersonal, and the grounds are in need of more greenery.

The hotel's restaurant, **AZZURA POINT**, (Moderate to Expensive), will be a high point of your visit, literally. This stunning dining room and lounge has loads of romantic promise for an intimate dinner and dancing above the bay.

Restaurant Kissing

CHEZ LOMA RESTAURANT, Coronado   ◆◆◆
1132 Loma Avenue
(619) 435-0661
Moderate

Take Orange Avenue to Loma Avenue and turn right to the restaurant.

Chez Loma is housed in a century-old Victorian cloaked in shades of pink and teal and bordered with a bright row of flower boxes. Inside, floral wallpaper blends nicely with fresh flower arrangements that fill the air with a faint sweetness. Chez Loma's award-winning cuisine is continental, its atmosphere is vibrant and unpretentious, making it a favorite for special celebrations and private tete-a-tetes.

◆ **Romantic Alternative: THE CHART HOUSE**, 1701 Strand Way, Coronado, (619) 435-0155, (Moderate), is one of the most charming places to dine waterside in Coronado. Built in 1887, this was once the boat house of the Hotel Del Coronado, thus its fanciful Victorian architecture and its location right out over the water. The atmosphere here is elegant without being stuffy. Its menu consists of fresh fish, meat, and poultry dishes, and the desserts are wonderful. However, it's the view of the docks and the Coronado Bridge that is bound to get most of your attention, besides the person you're with, that is.

PEOHE'S RESTAURANT, Coronado 💋
1201 First Street
(619) 437-4474
Moderate to Expensive

At the ferry landing in Coronado.

From the moment you step into Peohe's you may think the ferry that brought you here missed its destination and landed instead on someone's twisted idea of what a tropical island should look like. The decor here is best described as early Fijian or neo-Tahitian. The towering palm trees, trickling waterfalls, stone creeks filled with fish, and exotic flowers everywhere promote this South Sea Island deja vu. But a window seat will help you regain your orientation as you gaze out onto the downtown skyline reflected on the mirrored surface of the water. The view alone makes the gimmicks worth tolerating or enjoying, depending on your penchant for tropicana.

PRIMAVERA, Coronado
932 Orange Avenue
(619) 435-0454
Inexpensive to Moderate

The Coronado Bridge merges with Fourth Street. Take Fourth to Orange and turn left.

With all its splendor, Coronado seems to have one slight shortage: romantic dining. Primavera is a welcome exception. This elegant, sophisticated restaurant serves northern Italian cuisine in an intimate setting. It's a place where floral damask-covered booths are illuminated by dimly lit sconces and accented by dark woods. The pace is slow, the food is phenomenal, and the only thing more enticing than the dessert tray is the prospect of a moonlit stroll on the nearby shore.

◆ **Romantic Note:** Primavera's small bar area is partitioned by etched glass panels, but to ensure a quiet and cozy tryst, be sure to ask for a corner table or end booth on the other side of the restaurant.

Outdoor Kissing

BAY VIEW PARK, Coronado
At the corner of First and I streets.

This festive little park is such a well-kept secret that even many locals don't know it exists. Now it can be your secret as well, to share with someone special. However, if your definition of a park includes room to wander, you may want to find a different park. Bay View is about the size of a small house lot. In fact, that's what it was before the city turned it into an adorable knoll in the heart of a charming, albeit exclusive, neighborhood. The space is now filled by generous shade trees and inviting stone benches that look out onto the glittering bay and downtown skyline. It's an uncommon yet delightful place to confide words of love on a moonlit night.

Imperial Beach

Outdoor Kissing

HILLTOP STABLES, Imperial Beach   ❂❂❂
(619) 428-5441

CALIFORNIA HORSE RENTALS, Imperial Beach   ❂❂❂
(619) 428-5441

Call for directions.

You've seen it in plenty of movies: handsome young lovers riding horseback with a romantic ocean backdrop. But where on earth could you possibly do such a thing? Try that on most Southern California beaches and you'd trample half the population.

Then we heard about **BORDERFIELD STATE PARK**, the only beach in California where it's legal to ride horses. Both Hilltop Stables and California Horse Rentals can put you on a pony and head you in the right direction. It takes about 45 minutes to an hour to get to the beach from the stables, but once you reach the nature preserve's two and a half miles of sandy shores you are free to gallop in and out of the waves, the ocean breeze dancing in your hair. There's even a small corral to fence in the horses while you stop for an amorous seaside repast (picnic table provided). Whatever are you waiting for?

> *"Love expands; it not only sees more and enfolds more, it causes its object to bloom."*
> Hugh Prather

SAN DIEGO INLAND

Hotel/Bed and Breakfast Kissing

THE COTTAGE, Hillcrest
3829 Albatross Street
(619) 299-1564
Inexpensive

Located in a quiet canyon cul de sac, one block north of Robinson at Albatross.

The nice thing about The Cottage is you don't have to go over the river and through the woods to get to it. Instead, you'll find this quaint little home behind a home just a few blocks away from the heart of Hillcrest, an eclectic San Diego suburb filled with coffee shops and fine restaurants.

Built in 1913, The Cottage is reminiscent of a rustic Victorian cabin. There's a small sitting room complete with wood-burning stove and antique pump organ, a petite kitchen with gas stove and refrigerator, a full bath, and sleeping quarters where the bed takes up most of the room and mahogany paneling is accented by touches of emerald, burgundy, and blue. A TV is discreetly hidden behind a woven blind.

The cottage shares a wonderfully lush patio area with a guest room in the back of the main house. The *Garden Room* is beautifully decorated in emerald florals and has a private entry and bath. Guests are encouraged to unwind in the front parlor, enjoying the sounds of the working 1875 player organ, or thumb through the many books on art and opera. A continental breakfast is included in your stay, and the bread is always fresh from the oven.

THE HILL HOUSE, Golden Hills
2504 A Street
(619) 239-4738
Very Inexpensive to Expensive

Take Interstate 5 south and exit on Pershing Drive. Turn right at the light onto 26th Street. Go up the hill and turn right again at A Street.

The recession hasn't been kind to San Diego bed-and-breakfast inns: there aren't many left. Fortunately, the Hill House is still carrying on this fine tradition in grand style. From the moment you pass through the doors of this 1904 Dutch Colonial, you can sense the innkeepers' enormous dedication to making your stay unforgettable.

The Hill House is located near the downtown area, just minutes from the zoo, Balboa Park, and practically every other major attraction in town. Downstairs is a handsome parlor area adorned with antiques and warmed by a flickering fire. Upstairs, the four guest rooms all share the bathroom facilities (hence the plush terry robes furnished for each guest). Though this lack of privacy can be a downer, the rooms are uplifting. Each is quaint and cozy, reflective of days gone by. Lace curtains, homemade quilts, classic antiques, and windows seats combine to create a romantic ambience. Because it's the only room to come with a fireplace, the Hearthside is my favorite—there's nothing like cuddling by the fireside. On the third floor is a loft apartment with its own entrance, sun porch, bathroom, and kitchen facilities. It's decorated in a contemporary style and has two queen-size beds.

The lovely dining area, set with china and crystal, is the site of an expanded continental breakfast with a fresh fruit cup, hot-out-of-the-oven coffeecake or muffins, turkey sausages, and quiche or a baked egg dish. The owners will be happy to pack a gourmet picnic basket or surprise your loved one with flowers and champagne upon advance request. Romance is the nature of many bed and breakfasts, and Hill House is fiercely determined to uphold this noble legacy.

HORTON GRAND HOTEL, San Diego
311 Island Avenue
(619) 544-1886, (800) 999-1886
Moderate to Very Expensive

From Interstate 5 south take the Front Street exit (Front Street is one-way heading south) to Market Street and turn left. Proceed to Fourth Avenue, turn right, and go one block to the hotel.

The Horton Grand Hotel makes a travel writer's job a pleasure. The Horton is the result of a resourceful merging of two century-old hotels. Both were slated for demolition when an earnest and wise preservationist bought them from the city for a dollar apiece. Brick by brick, the hotels were dismantled and the materials were stored in a warehouse until finally, in 1986, a few blocks from the original site, they were resurrected side by side and connected by a courtyard with a glass atrium. Beyond the cheerful gingerbread facade is a sunny lobby sprinkled with Gatsby-style white wicker furniture and petite coffee tables. This is the site for a very traditional, very proper afternoon tea.

Up the winding oak staircase are 110 guest rooms, each individually decorated with antiques and charming touches of Victoriana (no two are alike). All come with private bathrooms and gas-burning fireplaces. Above the hearth, hidden in an antique-style cabinet, is a remote-control television provided for those who insist on living in the present. Most of the rooms have high ceilings and high platform beds, and many come with balconies overlooking the city lights or the atrium. The most romantic rooms are 214 and 216, poised above the courtyard's trickling fountain.

The hotel's **IDA BAILEY'S RESTAURANT** is named after the city's first female entrepreneur, a madam whose bordello was said to be located on this very spot. Like its namesake, the restaurant is lusty and sensual. A candlelight dinner here can prove to be positively sinful. The Sunday brunch on the sunny terrace is said to be the best in town. Of course, there's also something to be said for breakfast in bed—the choice is up to you.

◆   **Romantic Note:** When you make reservations here, be sure to specify the side of the hotel in which you'd like to stay. The left wing is more frilly and feminine; the right wing, once the Kahle Saddlery Hotel, has a more masculine ambience. Also, be sure to ask about their special-occasion packages. These promotional options not only save you money on the room rate but include wonderful extras such as a horse-drawn carriage ride, zoo tickets, or Sunday brunch at Ida Bailey's.

RANCHO VALENCIA, Rancho Santa Fe
5921 Valencia Circle
(619) 756-1123, (800) 548-3664
Very Expensive

From Interstate 5 take the Via de La Valle exit east to El Camino Real and turn right. At San Dieguito Road take a left and follow it to Rancho Dieguino Road. Turn right onto Rancho Dieguino Road, then take a quick left onto Rancho Valencia Road to the resort.

Rancho Valencia is San Diego's newest and finest luxury resort. Tucked away in the lush rolling hills of Rancho Santa Fe, this plush secluded hide-away has no "rooms," only suites in charming adobe cottages called *casitas*. Each lavish sanctuary has a vaulted ceiling, fireplace, wet bar, and a private garden terrace. The interiors are decorated in a crisp white-on-white Southwest style with pale pastel accents.

If you should decide to leave your casita you will find plenty of activities available. There are 18 tennis courts, cro-quet lawns, walking paths, a swimming pool, or you can have a massage. You can even rent a hot-air balloon for an exhilarating ride through the air. For a truly spectacular meal, try **LA TAPENADE,** (619) 756-1123, the resort's five-star restaurant, although for us it is a five lip celebration

U.S. GRANT HOTEL, San Diego
326 Broadway
(800) 334-6957
Expensive to Unbelievably Expensive

At the corner of Fourth and Broadway in downtown San Diego.

The luxurious lobby of the U.S. Grant Hotel is illuminated by enormous crystal chandeliers that will instantly bring your thoughts to the turn of the century, envisioning the days when this grand hotel first opened its highly polished mahogany doors. Dedicated to a former U.S. President by his son, it was once the haunt of dignitaries and movie stars. But perhaps the people who really appreciated the U.S. Grant the most were those who celebrated the most special days of their lives here: the lovers who dined in its spectacular restaurant; the brides and grooms who shared their first dance in its ornate ballrooms; the couples who celebrated anniversaries in its luxurious guest quarters.

Today, after an expansive renovation, the hotel is as spectacular as ever. Its guest rooms are furnished in Queen Anne reproductions and graced by stunning city views. Many of the hotel's suites offer a hydra-spa bath and fireplace. Afternoon tea in the lobby, accompanied by the lilt of soft piano music, is a nostalgic salute to the romance of yesteryear.

◆ **Romantic Alternative:** If you want elegance but don't need quite that much grandeur, consider the **HORTON PARK PLAZA HOTEL**, 520 E Street, San Diego, (800) 443-8012, (Moderate to Expensive). Like the U.S. Grant, this small 1917 luxury inn claims a small piece of San Diego history, but won't claim as much from your wallet. Its stately marble lobby, attractive rooms and suites, and beautiful city vistas combine to make it an intriguing substitute.

THE WESTGATE HOTEL, San Diego
1055 Second Avenue
(619) 238-1818, (800) 221-3802
Expensive to Unbelievably Expensive

In downtown San Diego, take Broadway to Third Avenue and go north. At the end of the street, a ramp on your right will take you to down into the valet parking area.

One should know ahead of time that there's nothing casual about the Westgate. It is ornate,18th-century European elegance personified, pure and simple.It's hard to believe the hotel is less than 20 years old. The service here is exemplary. The concierge will look after your every whim, your room will feature most every amenity, and a complimentary luxury car is at your service to drop you off at the airport, Sea World, the zoo, or any downtown location.

Then, just when you think it is safe to feel pampered, the Westgate ups the ante. **THE FOUNTAINBLEU ROOM,** (Moderate to Expensive), is the next best thing to dining in a castle. Gilded, flamboyant, and absolutely dripping with awards, it will treat you to an unforgettable culinary experience. The tuxedoed waiters are doting but a bit haughty (white gloves and all,) so think twice about dropping your fork here.

Restaurant Kissing

THE BELGIAN GARDEN, Mission Hills
808 West Washington Street
(619) 296-8010
Inexpensive to Moderate

From Interstate 5 take the Washington Street turnoff and head east. Not long after you reach the top of the hill, you'll see the restaurant on your left.

Though there are no medieval buildings here, no canals graced with long-necked swans, this quaint little restaurant is reminiscent of one you'd find on a cobblestoned Belgian street. Simple yet elegant, The Belgian Garden holds a scattering of tables embellished by wildflowers and surrounded by reminders of the old country: antique horns, copper kettles, Flemish oil paintings, and Belgian lace curtains.

The food is continental and the service is warm and friendly. The exquisite desserts will keep you coming back for more. But perhaps the best thing about this well-kept secret is the little niche the owners have affectionately dubbed the Brussels Room, an intimate nook set off by a mock wall partition with real windows, curtains, and paintings. These embellishments serve to accentuate its detachment from the rest of the restaurant and the rest of the world.

BUSALACCHI'S RESTAURANT, Hillcrest
3683 Fifth Avenue
(619) 298-0119
Moderate to Expensive

On Fifth Avenue, between Anderson and Pennsylvania streets.

Busalacchi's is divided into a half-dozen tiny sections, each aglow with candlelight and intimate detailing. You can dine in front of a flickering fireplace, by a lace-covered window, or on the enclosed terrace. This was once a private home, and it has maintained that intimate atmosphere. The air is fragrant with Italian spices and aromas of Sicilian specialties. Busalacchi's is a favorite of even the most finicky critics, and though I'm usually not guilty of eavesdropping I couldn't help but overhear the couple next to me singing its praises as well: "Being here always takes me back to Europe and some of our more torrid nights there." Enough said.

◆ **Romantic Alternative**: Right next door is another fabulous restaurant that dishes up romance Italian-style. **STEPHANO'S**, 3671 Fifth Avenue, San Diego, (619) 296-0975, (Moderate), doesn't have the homey, intimate feeling that Busalacchi's has, but is a wonderfully elegant alternative.

CAFE DEL REY MORO, Balboa Park
1549 El Prado
(619) 234-8511
Inexpensive to Moderate

Take the Sasafras Street exit off Interstate 5, and turn left on Laurel. Follow Laurel into the heart of Balboa Park, where the street veers off to the right. You will see a statue of El Cid; the cafe is to the left of the statue.

This lovely Mexican/Southwestern restaurant may be one of the ultimate places to kiss in San Diego—at least to kiss and say "I do." Over the past 50 years, thousands of couples have chosen the cascading terraces of Cafe del Rey Moro as their wedding site, where its wishing well and lily pond are the receptacles for many a hopeful coin toss. Walking down the aisle is not a prerequisite for visiting Cafe del Rey Moro, however. You need only be hungry and in search of a place for quiet conversation on a sun-drenched terrace overflowing with flowers and surrounded by towering trees. Don't be surprised, though, if you hear a wedding march and glimpse a bride and groom below. Blossoming love and blossoming flora make this a great place to kiss, whether or not the minister has instructed you to do so.

CAFE LULU, San Diego   ◆◆◆◆
417 F Street
(619) 238-0114
Inexpensive to Moderate

Call for directions.

To call Cafe Lulu stunning would almost do it an injustice. This up-scale cappuccino bar, decorated more like a modern art gallery than a coffeehouse, is truly a treat for the eyes. As you enter, notice the mirror-glass-and-tone collage at your feet, the gilded mirror, the large exotic bouquet, and the interesting blend of rippled glass and neon light in the far corner. While offering the kind of items found in most coffee-houses, such as desserts, baked goods, and light breakfast items, the menu also boasts such tantalizing items such as raspberry baked Brie. Situated near the heart of the Gaslamp Quarter, this is a great place to start or end your evening.

CELADON, Hillcrest   ◆◆◆
3628 Fifth Street
(619) 295-8800
Inexpensive

Call for directions.

Celadon can add spice to a romantic evening. Thai food is renowned (and revered) for its flamboyant flavors: sweet, sour, hot, spicy. Just the thought can bring tears to your eyes. But these are tears of joy. You will have a lovely and romantic dining experience.

Celadon blushes in the palest shade of pink. The dining room is enhanced by touches of blue, gray, and green, and highlights this alluring palette with well-chosen impressionistic prints, oversized Oriental pots bursting with colorful silk bouquets, and antique tapestries. The menu includes such tempting dishes such as shrimp in spicy coconut cream and chicken curry. If you and your companion savor spicy food, then Celadon can indeed heat up the evening.

CHANG, La Mesa ◆◆◆◆
5500 Grossmont Center Drive, Grossmont Center
(619) 464-2288
Inexpensive to Moderate

From Interstate 8, take the Grossmont Center Drive turnoff. Chang is on the north side of the shopping center.

It seems unimaginable that one of San Diego's most engaging treasures is in a shopping mall, but it is. Chang is a great find, full of pleasing paradoxes. The decor is somewhat high-tech, yet the ambience is soft and romantic. The steel blue leather booths are subdued by floral embroidered panels and blush-colored linens. Dimly lit sconces illuminate every table, but the pink neon that encircles the ceiling is what casts an enchanting glow upon the room. If you arrive and exit through the private entrance off the parking lot you'll hardly notice the commercial surroundings.

The menu is traditional Cantonese from the cashew chicken to the Peking duck and butterfly shrimp. Every dish is beautifully prepared, and at these prices your meal won't take the romance out of your evening.

◆ **Romantic Note:** Chang also has a La Jolla location in the Costa Verde Center, on Genesee at La Jolla Village Drive, (619) 558-2288.

DANSK TEA ROOM, La Mesa   ❦❦
8425 La Mesa Boulevard
(619) 463-0640
Inexpensive

Call for directions.

If you think tenderly of gingerbread cottages with lace curtains and are craving to discover a breakfast spot designed with the sweet tooth in mind, then you will want to discover the Dansk Tea Room. As you may expect, the interior is traditional Scandinavian, in blue and white, with Royal Copenhagen pottery lining its walls. You can dine on sumptuous treats: paper-thin Swedish pancakes loaded with powdered sugar and lingonberries, omelets filled with Danish sausage and smothered in red wine sauce, crispy Belgian waffles overflowing with fruit, and homemade cranberry bread are just a few of the choices. If the sugar gets to be too much, the tea room also serves lunch and a traditional Swedish or Danish smorgasbord upon request.

EL BIZCOCHO, Rancho Bernardo   ❦❦❦
17550 Bernardo Oaks Drive, Rancho Bernardo Inn
(619) 487-1611
Expensive

From Interstate 15, take the Rancho Bernardo Road exit and head east. Turn left onto Bernardo Oaks Drive.

El Bizcocho is a restaurant of interesting contradictions. Despite its Spanish name and California mission design, it offers first-class French nouvelle cuisine. The tables here are so well spaced and the room so warm and endearing, a couple could feel as though they have this sizable place all to themselves. The service is attentive yet inconspicuous. But more than anything else, El Bizcocho is a good place to kiss. Its enormous picture windows peer out onto a lush golf course and stately hillside homes. By dusk, its subtle peach decor takes on a dreamy golden glow.

◆ **Romantic Note:** Reservations are suggested and jackets are required.

JAVA, San Diego
837 G Street
(619) 235-4012
Inexpensive

Java, located in downtown San Diego, is like other espresso bars in the area. But be warned, in some ways this is a completely different animal. Java is home to an artsy and eclectic crowd, ranging from punks in mohawks to yuppies in business attire. In addition to being an art gallery and a home for wayward poets (they feature a poetry reading once a month), Java has one of the most diverse coffee menus I've yet come across, each selection named after a famous artist or writer.

MOLLY'S, San Diego
333 West Harbor
(619) 234-1500
Moderate to Expensive

At the corner of Front and First streets.

Molly's will exceed all your expectations for a perfect evening. The food is exquisite and the service flawless. The room is resplendent with dark wood paneling, emerald green velvet chairs, and marble accents. Each booth or table is separated by a softly lit beveled glass panel. Bottled Vittel water is the standard complimentary offering when you sit down and the pianist gladly takes requests.

Caesar salad, steaks, and seafood are all sensational, beautifully presented and delicious. Dessert coffee is a regal production served on a silver platter with all the trimmings: shaved chocolate, orange peel and whipped cream flavored with amaretto. The desserts are equally grand, while the dark chocolate truffles and chocolate-dipped strawberries served at the end of your meal are sublime.

MR. A'S RESTAURANT, San Diego
2550 Fifth Avenue
(619) 239-1377
Expensive to Moderate

At the top of the Fifth Avenue Financial Center, on the corner of Laurel and Fifth.

Mr. A's is San Diego's classic destination for intimate dining, as much a part of the city's personality as Balboa Park, which it soars above. This place is expensive, opulent, possibly even garish, but when your date takes you here, you know something serious is at hand.

The restaurant is decorated in deep burgundy, accented by rich wood trim and embellished by elaborate golden candelabras. On most nights, the aisles are packed with tableside carts at which the waiters flambe practically everything. Fortunately, Mr. A's is not all flash. Its continental cuisine is award-winning and the wine list extensive. The maitre d' was almost giddy as he told us about a rare 1963 vintage. The real claim to fame here, though, is the view, an unparalleled vista of the city. You can enjoy it from virtually any seat in the restaurant or while sipping a romantic nightcap in the cocktail lounge.

PREGO, Mission Valley
1370 Frazee Road
(619) 294-4700
Inexpensive to Moderate

Prego is in the Hazard Center, just east of Highway 163 at Mission Gorge.

Prego is one of the new breed of trattorias that have popped up all over the city. Elegant and sophisticated, they offer delectable, beautifully presented Italian cuisine. From the outside, Prego looks like a grand country villa. Behind its wrought-iron gate, you'll find a romantic patio enhanced by a bubbling fountain and vine-covered walls. The inside is large, with plenty of intimate nooks and corners. Wonderful smells emanate from the open kitchen, and it's easy to second-guess your order as you watch the waiter pass with someone else's food. Everything looks so appealing! The menu consists primarily of pastas and gourmet pizzas, but includes a variety of tasty fish and meat dishes as well.

◆ **Romantic Alternatives**: Other local trattorias include **TUTTE MARE**, 4365 Executive Drive, San Diego, (619) 597-1188, in the Golden Triangle, and **PIATTI**, 2182 Avenida de la Playa, San Diego, (619) 454-1589, near the La Jolla Shores. Both restaurants follow the same delicious recipe for success, and succeed quite nicely. Tutte Mare is the more romantic of the two, but a garden table at Piatti assures you of an enchanting evening enhanced by sea breezes and unforgettable food.

QUAILS INN, San Marcos
1035 La Bonita Drive
(619) 744-2445
Moderate to Expensive

Take Highway 78 to the Rancho Santa Fe exit. Go south two miles and take a left on Lake San Marcos. Follow the signs to the inn.

Quails Inn lies alongside beautiful **LAKE SAN MARCOS**, bustling by day with water taxis, shimmering at night with moonbeams and the elongated shadows of the houses set above it. That makes it the perfect spot for a lingering cocktail in the lounge or a satisfying dinner at a window table. The menu is primarily steak, chicken, and fish, with an elaborate salad bar and a sumptuous Sunday brunch.

◆ **Romantic Note**: San Marcos is a popular retirement community. Let this inspire you: romance can blossom at any age.

RAINWATER'S, San Diego

1202 Kettner Boulevard
(619) 233-5757
Moderate to Expensive

PACIFICA GRILL, San Diego
1202 Kettner Boulevard
(619) 696-9226
Moderate

On Kettner Boulevard between A and B streets.

Rainwater's and Pacifica Grill are part of a three-story complex that houses several art galleries and these two superb restaurants. Rainwater's is dark, sensuous, and adorned by city lights. It is truly a stately place to dine. There is terrace seating that looks down upon the rest of the complex. Follow its suspended staircase to the top and you'll discover a room that is illuminated by little more than candlelight. Once settled into a large cozy booth, your adventure in fine dining will begin. Primarily, a steak house, Rainwater's also dabbles in seafood and pasta, and their desserts are divine.

Downstairs is where you'll find Pacifica Grill. They serve American Southwest cuisine in a soft romantic atmosphere. The seafood entrees are particularly fresh and tantalizing. The views from this dining location aren't as spectacular as Rainwater's, but the food and surroundings more than make up for that.

Outdoor Kissing

BALBOA PARK, San Diego

Take Laurel Street east from Interstate 5 and you'll end up right in the heart of the park.

Balboa Park is a romantic adventure waiting to happen, and you don't have to spend a cent in order to come home with a fortune in memories. The 1,400 acres of lush tropical greenery seem to be perpetually in bloom. Perhaps that is why almost everyone has a smile and every couple walking hand-in-hand looks misty-eyed. Even the sidewalk performers seem disinterested in the coins they've collected during their act, satisfied just with the joy of being there.

No matter how many times you've been here, there's always new territory to explore. It takes hours to stroll the entire grounds, days to see everything in the celebrated zoo, weeks to explore its 11 museums. There are organ concerts to be heard, international cottages to investigate, and plays to attend at its three theaters. A tour of the botanical gardens, followed by a picnic at the reflecting pool, a kiss at the wishing well, and even a ride on an old-fashioned carousel make for an idyllic afternoon. A day of exploration at Balboa Park will make you feel that you've grabbed the brass ring.

CORONADO FERRY, San Diego
1050 North Harbor Drive
(619) 234-4111
Coronado places are listed in the San Diego Coast Chapter.

At the foot of Broadway and North Harbor Drive.

Although Coronado is just a short drive across the bay from the downtown embarcadero, getting there by ferry makes the trip much more romantic. For $2 each you can leave the car behind, take along a couple of bikes, and head out in search of an unforgettable day. The trip takes only 15 minutes, but it's 15 minutes of gliding across shimmering waters filled with sailboats and catamarans, taking in wonderful skyline views. Though the boat is often crowded, there's not a spot on board where you can't feel the sun on your face or the wind in your hair.

◆ **Romantic Note:** The ferries leave downtown every hour on the hour, starting at 9 A.M. The last boat returns from Coronado at 10:30 P.M. weeknights, 11:30 P.M. weekends.

◆ **Romantic Suggestion:** While you are at the ferry landing, why not take a leisurely stroll on the boardwalk? There are shops to snoop in, fresh chocolate chip cookies to munch, and, on weekends, performances by strolling minstrels and jazz artists. The nearby grass is soft and the view of the harbor is magnificent.

DEER PARK, Escondido
29013 Champagne Boulevard
(619) 749-1666

Take the Deer Springs exit from Interstate 15. Head east to Champagne Boulevard and turn left. The park is about three miles up the road, on the right-hand side.

I was excited when I heard about this orchard, said to be full of picturesque, unspoiled areas designed for dreamy, peaceful picnicking. But when I drove up to Deer Park and discovered a market/deli/car museum, I felt a sinking sensation. It all seemed so touristy and tacky. I continued on, hoping that there was more to the park than this. My patience paid off; the Deer Park general store is really just a stop on your way to a sublime afternoon.

After a little wine tasting at the deli, you can pick out your favorite, ask them to pack you a picnic lunch, and then gain free access to the grounds. You may want to spread out a blanket under the shade of an enormous sycamore tree or claim a picnic bench next to the spiraling vines. This is a wonderful country hideaway just minutes from the city.

◆ **Romantic Note:** You may know that Deer Park is the name of a winery in Napa Valley. This location, though not a winery itself, is a satellite outlet for its Napa Valley sister.

EMBARCADERO MARINA PARK, San Diego

Take Harbor Drive to Fifth Avenue and head south until it dead-ends at the park.

A couple of blocks east of Seaport Village and right next to the Intercontinental Hotel is a pretty little park that until recently was a wonderfully well-kept secret. However, like it or not, the San Diego Convention Center has become its newest neighbor, and only time will tell whether conventioneers will stumble onto its pristine shores. The Embarcadero Marina Park is a peninsula-like stretch of land that lies practically in the shadow of the Coronado Bridge, looking out onto the docks and a bay overflowing with boats and catamarans. The park has a small pier, a quaint gazebo, plenty of hungry sea gulls to feed, and even a workout path that winds around its stretch of shoreline. But while a sit-up here and a pull-up there may be invigorating, most couples seem content just to spread out a blanket and smooch, which can also be a heart-healthy activity.

GASLAMP QUARTER, San Diego

The Gaslamp Quarter extends from Broadway to L Street and from Fourth to Sixth Avenues. The most popular nightspots seems to be on Fifth Avenue between E and F streets.

The Gaslamp Quarter is where you'll encounter the history and nightlife of San Diego. Restored to turn-of-the-century authenticity, the streets are crowded with people, lined with jazz clubs, and filled with restaurants. You can dance the night away, listen to the sultry blues of a local artist, or simply wander the area sightseeing. This is San Diego's most lively nightspot.

◆ **Romantic Suggestions:** **FIO'S**, 801 Fifth Avenue, (619) 234-3467, (Inexpensive to Moderate), offers delicious Italian cuisine in beautiful, chic surroundings. **FALCO**, 835 Fifth Avenue, (619) 233-5687, (Moderate to Expensive), has a classic romantic atmosphere enhanced by crystal chandeliers, crisp white linens, and silver vases containing a single rose. The food is an innovative blend of European and California techniques and ingredients. **CROCE'S**, 802 Fifth Avenue, (619) 233-4355, (Moderate), is named after the late singer/songwriter Jim Croce. More up tempo than the other restaurants in the area, this attractive spot features sidewalk dining, international cuisine, and live jazz. Its sister restaurant, **INGRID'S CANTINA**, 822 Fifth Avenue, (619) 233-6945, (Moderate), offers American Southwest entrees and live rhythm and blues from its adjoining **TOP HAT** nightclub. There are also a few coffee bars in the Quarter, as well as **THE INSOMNIAC**, 820 Fifth, (619) 239-5320 (Moderate), an espresso bar/gallery/theater/nightclub with a varied musical repertoire.

MOUNT HELIX, La Mesa

Take Fuerte Drive south from Interstate 8. Turn right onto Mount Helix Drive and follow the road to the top of the mountain.

Mount Helix at one time was the city's passion pit (or peak, depending on your perspective), the place you went to see the submarine races. Times have changed and it is no longer the relatively innocent place it once was. Now the park is closed after sunset and you can't even drive to the top anymore because the road is barricaded. The good news is that Mount Helix is still worth the trip. The views of San Diego and the El Cajon Valley are sensational, and on a clear day it's a dramatic spot to take in a sunset. There are plenty of stony crags on which to sit and ponder the universe (by day), or you can picnic at the top of the amphitheater if your concerns are less metaphysical.

Perhaps the best thing about Mount Helix is that it's still a prime spot to watch love in bloom. Two by two, people of all ages come here to appreciate the countryside and each other, knowing they're sharing in something that makes life just a little more special.

THE SAN DIEGO ZOO, Balboa Park
(619) 234-3153

At Park Boulevard and Zoo Place.

The San Diego Zoo is not only one of the largest zoos in the world, it's one of the most beautiful. Spanning 100 acres of lush greenery and exotic flora, the zoo is home to more than 3,500 animals. With too much to see in just one day, you might want to cuddle up on the double-decker bus tour, enjoy a bird's-eye view from the Skyfari Aerial Tram, or go it by foot along the zoo's verdant and winding trails. If you consider zoos to be places for kids and tourists only, you are in for a big surprise. A visit with the wild and gentle animals who share the earth with us is as enriching and joyous as anything in San Diego. Besides, what better way than a day at the zoo to bring out the animal in each of us?

SEAPORT VILLAGE, San Diego
849 West Harbor Drive
(619) 235-4014

From Interstate 5 take the Airport exit, which merges with Kettner. Follow Kettner south and it will lead right to Seaport Village.

Shopping might make my heart beat a bit faster, but it makes most men anxious and irritable. Seaport Village is different. This 14-acre specialty park on the bay is filled with 85 quaint New England-style shops offering everything from mugs to music boxes, cookies to crystal. And this is one shopping center that offers more than just a way to spend your money. Scattered between the brightly colored shops are babbling brooks, weeping willows, and flower-covered knolls. Mimes and magicians steal smiles from the passersby, sidewalk vendors sell caramel apples and colorful balloons, and a century-old hand-carved carousel offers rides to kids of all ages. On top of all this, there's the glistening bay and a sky dancing with colorful kites being flown in the small adjacent park.

While you could make it through an afternoon without purchasing anything more than a box of popcorn, it's just as easy to munch your way from one end of the park to the other. There are 13 diverse eateries here, but the discriminating romantic may want to wait for a window seat at one of the park's four bayside restaurants. **PAPAGUYO'S**, 861 West Harbor Drive, (619) 232-7581, (Moderate), is a perfect seafood restaurant with Mexican flair, decorated in soothing ocean tones of pinkish coral and seafoam green. The dining area is divided into two levels so everyone can share equally in the picture-postcard view. More casual, yet also quite tempting, is the **SAN DIEGO PIER CAFE**, 885 West Harbor Drive, (619) 239-3968, (Inexpensive to Moderate), a New England-style boathouse set on stilts above the water.

Enjoy a dessert and cappuccino at **UPSTART CROW**, 835 West Harbor Drive, (619) 232-4855, (Inexpensive). With a backdrop like Seaport Village, Upstart Crow has to be wonderful and it is. This combination bookstore/coffeehouse is a popular hangout for tourists and locals alike. They feature the usual offering of coffees, delicious desserts and baked goods, but I think what draws most people is the opportunity to browse through the many books as well.

◆   **Romantic Suggestion:** A great way to tour downtown in style is to take a **CINDERELLA CARRIAGE RIDE,** 801 West Market Street, San Diego, (619) 239-8080. The old-fashioned horse-drawn carriages, right out of a fairy tale, can usually be found in front of the Harbor House at Seaport Village. Given some notice, they will be happy to whisk you off from any downtown hotel or restaurant. The ride costs $40 for 30 minutes, $60 for an hour.

"For a moment each seemed unreal to the other... then the slow warm hum of love began."
F. Scott Fitzgerald

"Our deepest feelings live in words unspoken."
Flavia

WORTH THE TRIP
FROM SAN DIEGO

Julian

Take Interstate 8 east to Highway 79 north and head into the town of Julian.

For Southern Californians, the town of Julian in the Cleveland National Forest is a special getaway. This old mining site, set high in the Vallecito Mountains, serves as a reminder of days long past. Things move at a slower pace out here, the skies are a bit bluer, and the mountain air is a lot fresher. The drive alone is worth the trip: coiling backroads take you through pine-covered meadows, past blossoming orchards, and around Lake Cuyamaca. A century ago people made the trek to Julian in search of gold; nowadays folks come here seeking peace and quiet, both of which can be found in ample supply. Did I forget to mention that this area is also famous for its apples? Apple pie a la mode and fresh cider will be the first of your pleasant discoveries here. The rest is up to you.

Bed and Breakfast Kissing

BUTTERFIELD BED AND BREAKFAST, Julian
2284 Sunset Drive
(619) 765-2179
Inexpensive to Moderate

Take Highway 79 headed toward Borrego and turn right on Whispering Pines Road. Turn right again on Sunset.

Butterfield is the other side of Alice's looking glass; there's a touch of Wonderland here. To start with, you can actually sleep in the bed used in the television taping of *Alice in Wonderland*. Beautiful and ornate, it blends easily into its new surroundings, for everything at Butterfield is wonderfully whimsical.

The inn is nestled in the pine-covered hills of Julian, about a mile outside of town. It's close enough to hike there, but far enough from civilization to have the makings of a fanciful mountain retreat. Once inside this cozy home, you'll discover a hearth guarded by teddy bears, huge feather-nest beds, and comfortable bay window seats that peek out onto the lovely meadows below. Choose from four charming rooms, each sharing an adjoining bath, or for a little more privacy, try the delightful *Christmas Cottage*, decked for the holidays year-round. The gourmet breakfast here is remarkable; enjoy this special treat in the garden gazebo when summer warms the mountain air, or before the crackling hearth in the cold of winter.

◆ **Romantic Alternative:** If you love the bed-and-breakfast experience but don't like sharing it with so many other people, try **PINECROFT MANOR**, 2142 Whispering Pines, Julian, (619) 765-1611, (Inexpensive). This English tudor house has only two guest rooms and pampers its guests in true British style.

JULIAN HOTEL, Julian
2032 Main Street
(619) 765-0201
Inexpensive to Expensive

Take Highway 8 east to the Highway 79/Julian exit. From there, it's about a half-hour drive into town. The hotel is in the heart of the city on the right-hand side.

Stepping into the Julian Hotel is like stepping back into another time. This hotel is nearly a century old and little about it has changed since its opening in 1897. The walls seem to whisper of the days when the rooms were filled with Victorian twosomes who sipped tea in the parlor, strolled through the gardens, and walked arm-in-arm down hallways barely wide enough to accommodate all those lacy petticoats. Today patrons come here to escape the workaday world and lose themselves in a place where phones don't seem to exist. There are 16 rather small but charming guest chambers and a separate honeymoon cottage behind the hotel. In the morning, fresh fruit, eggs Florentine, and Dudley's bread await you in the parlor.

◆ **Romantic Warning:** Most of the rooms share bathroom facilities, which means you've got to take a trip down the hall on occasion, but in the name of authenticity it just might be worth it.

◆ **Romantic Suggestion:** Down the street and around the corner from the Julian Hotel is a wonderful alternative for young parents determined to find romance in spite of the kids. **JULIAN FARMS LODGING,** 2818 Washington Street, Julian, (619) 765-0250, (Inexpensive), has only four rooms; they are much bigger than those at the Julian Hotel and have the same cozy Victorian charm. Each comes with a private bath and a sitting room with a twin bed for the little one. Lodging here is fairly inexpensive, which means it's usually booked well in advance.

THE JULIAN WHITE HOUSE, Julian
3014 Blue Jay Drive
(619) 765-1764
Moderate

From the heart of Julian, take Highway 78/79 in the direction of Ramona. Turn left on Pine Hills Road and take another left at Blue Jay Drive.

The Julian White House is a throwback to the days of Tara. It is a beautiful mansion with stately white pillars and a sweeping veranda where afternoon tea is served. In the cozy parlor, classical music fills the air. Each of the guest rooms is filled with elegant country touches, but unfortunately all but one share a bath. In the morning a gourmet breakfast is served in the dining room.

RANDOM OAKS RANCH, Julian   ❖●❖❮
3742 Pine Hills Road
(619) 765-1094
Moderate

Call for directions.

There are several wonderful bed and breakfasts here in Julian to choose from, but this one has something special: a brand-new, exquisitely decorated cottage.

The ranch is a mile or two outside of town in a pretty wooded area abundant with fragrant pine and shade trees. Wildflowers are scattered throughout. Although this is a horse ranch, the beautiful creatures are here for guests to pet, not ride. That's OK, though; the occasional whinny adds to the feeling that you are far from home. There are two guest cottages to choose from: Country Oaks, a quaint bungalow complete with its own kitchen and bath, and the resplendent new English Squire Cottage, elegant from start to finish.

The English Squire Cottage is paneled with mahogany and decorated in hunter green and filled with flawless antiques. The wood-burning fireplace can be enjoyed from the partially canopied bed, crisp with snow-white Battenburg linens. The bathroom and shower are as elegant as anything you'd find at the Ritz Carlton, and come with thick, comfy robes for two.

While guests in both cabins receive the same warm hospitality, those in the English Squire are treated to a few indulgent extras: gourmet beans for the coffeepot and a sample bottle of the local Mendehini wine, and the extensive heart-healthy breakfast is not only brought to their room but actually laid out and served in their private dining nook.

◆ **Romantic Alternative:** Not far from Random Oaks Ranch nestled among the pines, **MOUNTAIN HIGH BED AND BREAKFAST**, 4110 Deer Lake Park Road, Julian, (619) 765-1083, (Moderate), has a cute cottage, complete with kitchen facilities, and a small but secluded room tucked in the back of the main house. Both come with private baths and entries, a fireplace, TV/VCR, and a full breakfast. True to its name, Mountain High is located on a hill in a majestic stretch of privately owned forest. The double hammock stretched between enormous Ponderosa pines looks like a promising place to curl up and kiss!

SHADOW MOUNTAIN RANCH, Julian
2771 Frisius Road
(619) 765-0323
Inexpensive to Moderate

Take Highway 78 north from town and turn left on Pine Hills Road. In about three miles, turn right onto Frisius Road.

Shadow Mountain Ranch is the product of an overactive imagination. On the one hand it is an authentic dude ranch with horses, cattle, ducks, and chicks; on the other hand it's an inn where the rooms are filled with waggery and whimsy. One room has a secret passage that leads to the hot tub. There's also a tree house built for two, though its open toilet is sure to give modest people nightmares. Or consider the Enchanted Cottage, a Bavarian bungalow complete with an arched wooden doorway, a wood-burning stove, and a snuggly bay window seat overlooking the meadows. There are eight guest rooms in all, including a new structure the owners have proudly dubbed the Gnome Home. (This one you've got to see for yourself.) A stay here comes with a hearty ranch breakfast, afternoon tea, and a complimentary glass of sherry or warm vanilla milk at the end of the day. There are plenty of trails to hike and trees to climb, so feel free to let the kid in you go wild—it's never too late to become childhood sweethearts.

◆ **Romantic Note:** Regrettably, the ranch's horses are for looking at, not riding. Also, you have to book far in advance if you want to get a reservation at this popular location.

Restaurant Kissing

JULIAN GRILLE, Julian
2224 Main Street
(619) 765-0173
Moderate

In the heart of town, just past the grocery store.

The Julian Grille represents the most endearing aspects of this mountain town. The atmosphere here is warm, cozy, and inviting, yet there is an underlying elegance. The restaurant itself is located in a 1910 country building that is aglow with twinkling lights.

The dining area still has the homey feeling of the grange it once was, but the classical music and pink linens lend a more stately mood. A table near the flickering hearth or by a lace-covered window in the enclosed patio promises an enjoyable evening enhanced by good food, loving conversation, and delightful memories of the alpine getaway you both desperately needed.

◆   **Romantic Suggestion:** There aren't many restaurants in Julian, especially romantic ones, but **ROMANO'S DODGE HOUSE RES-TAURANT**, 2718 B Street, (619) 765-1003, (Inexpensive to Moderate), is definitely the coziest hideaway in town. It's a log-cabin-style diner with lace curtains, checkered tablecloths, and a zesty Italian menu.

Outdoor Kissing

COUNTRY CARRIAGES, Julian
P.O. Box 607
(619) 876-1471

Call for prices and pickup locations.

For Southern Californians accustomed to surf and sun, this is a winter fantasy come true. Imagine whisking down a snow-covered mountain road in an old-fashioned horse-drawn carriage. Snuggled close together, you hold hands beneath a fluffy down quilt while a brisk mountain breeze nips at your cheeks. Yes, in the town of Julian, an hour's drive from the coast, nature wears white in the winter. Of course, you can take advantage of a romantic carriage ride in Julian any time of year. Most couples choose to be picked up from their hotel or bed and breakfast, dropped off for dinner, then swept off once again for a moonlit drive. The ride lasts less than an hour; the memories will surely last a lifetime.

Temecula

Vineyards draping sun-drenched hillsides, hot-air balloons filling the skies with crayon-bright color, connoisseurs sipping wine in a provocative stone courtyard—these are what you'll find throughout the Temecula wine country. And while this may not be Napa Valley, the hills here are bursting with sweeping vistas and ripening grapes. The best part is that it's only an hour's drive from San Diego and Los Angeles, although the atmosphere is worlds away.

LOMA VISTA BED AND BREAKFAST, Temecula
33350 La Serena Way
(714) 676-7047
Moderate

Call for directions.

Loma Vista Bed and Breakfast is nestled in the heart of the Southern California wine country. The attractive mission-style hacienda is probably too contemporary to be considered endearing or cozy, but it is decorated with personality and charm. Several of the rooms have private balconies that look out onto the citrus groves and vineyards that blanket the valley. Loma Vista is also minutes from downtown Temecula, a colorful (though somewhat touristy) frontier town decked out in Western garb. Your stay here includes a generous champagne breakfast buffet served in the dining room or flower-clad garden patio, and nightly cheese and wine tasting in the living room.

Restaurant Kissing

CAFE CHAMPAGNE, Temecula   ❤❤❤❤
Culbertson Winery
32575 Rancho California Road
(714) 699-0088
Moderate to Expensive

Take the Rancho California turnoff from I-15. Head south; the winery will be on your right.

Cafe Champagne, part of the Culbertson Winery, is perhaps the valley's premier distraction. After a day of wine tasting or hiking through the verdant valleys and hills, this is the perfect place to let it all soak in. The Mediterranean-style villa is right out of a French movie, cascading stone fountain and all. The interior has a traditional European country mood that is both elegant and comfortable. The cobblestone courtyard is the best spot for an intimate afternoon or evening meal, with a terrace that looks out over the abundant vineyards. Not surprisingly, the continental cuisine here is designed to complement the wines and champagnes. A leisurely evening in this lovely restaurant promises to leave you both feeling as bubbly as a newly opened bottle of champagne.

PERSONAL DIARY

This is the section just for the two of you, so you can keep your own record of the romantic moments you've shared together. Keeping a record of special times, to read when the moment is right, can be an adoring gift, when another romantic outing is at hand.

INDEX

A

A Balloon Ride Adventure, 82
Air Affaire Enterprises, 82
Alice's Restaurant, 53
Alisal, The, 17
Allegro, 30
Amelia's 102
Anaheim, 91
Angeles Crest Highway, 80
Angeles National Forest, 80
Arrowhead Queen, 136
Azzura Point, 186

B

Balboa, 100
Balboa Inn, 100
Balboa Island, 103
Balboa Park, 204
Balboa Pavillion and Fun Zone, 103
Ballard, 18
Ballard Inn, 18
Ballard Store Restaurant and Bar, 19
Bay View Park, 188
Bayberry Inn, 23
Beach House, 10
Beau Rivage, 54
Bed and Breakfast Inn at La Jolla, 165
Belgian Garden, 196
Belgian Lion, 182
Belgian Waffle Works, 136
Belmont Park, 180
Belvedere, 49
Bernadette's, 36
Bernard's, 39
Bernini's, 166
Big Bear Lake, 132

Biltmore, The, 39
Bistro Gardens, 54
Bistro Restaurant, 55
Blue Dolphin Inn, 11
Blue Lantern Inn, 116
Blue Quail Inn, 24
Blue Whale Inn, 12
Boat and Breakfast, 183
Borderfield State Park, 189
Brasserie Restaurant, 47
Bravo! Barcelone, 167
Brea, 91
Brigantine Restaurant, 159
Brigitte's, 31
Britta's Cafe, 101
Busalacchi's Restaurant, 197
Butler's Grill, 42
Butterfield Bed and Breakfast, 213
Butterfields's, 55
Byron Vineyards, 20

C

Cafe 928, 167
Cafe Champagne, 220
Cafe Court, 39
Cafe Del Mar, 159
Cafe Del Rey Moro, 197
Cafe Des Artistes, 56
Cafe Lulu, 198
Cafe Mondrian and Lounge, 57
California Horse Rentals, 189
Californian, The, 116
Cambria, 9
Camille's, 57
Cannons, 119
Capistrano, 120

Capistrano Seaside Inn, 120
Captain Don's, 35
Cardiff-by-the-Sea, 153
Cardiff-by-the-Sea Bed and
    Breakfast, 153
Cardiff-by-the-Sea Lodge, 154
Carlos and Pepe's, 58
Carlsbad, 150
Carlsbad Inn, 151
Carriage House, Lake Arrowhead, 132
Carriage House, Laguna Beach, 105
Casa de Flores, 122
Casa Laguna Inn, 106
Casa Tropicana, 123
Castaways, 58
Casual Elegance, 140
Catalina Cruises, 125
Catalina Express, 125
Catalina Holiday Passenger Service, 125
Catalina Island, 125
Cedar Creek Inn, 110
Celadon, 198
Cellar, The, 91
Century City Inn, 39
Century Plaza Hotel Tower, 40
Chandler Pavilion, 39
Chang, 199
Channel Islands, 34
Channel Road Inn, 40
Charlie's Grill, 155
Charlton Flats, 80
Chart House, Coronado, 187
Chart House, Dana Point, 119
Chateau du Lac Bed and Breakfast, 132
Checkers Hotel Kempinski, 41
Checkers Restaurant, 41
Cheshire Cat, 24
Chesterfield, 42
Chez Helene, 59
Chez Loma Restaurant, 186

Cinderella Carriage Ride, 210
Cinegrill Lounge, 63
Citronell Restaurant, 31
Claes', 108
Cold Creek Canyon Preserve, 86
Colette, 59
Corona Del Mar, 104
Coronado, 184
Coronado Ferry, 205
Cottage Restaurant, 168
Cottage, The Hill Crest, 191
Cottage, The Laguna Beach, 110
Country Carriages, 218
Crescent Bay Point Park, 115
Croce's, 207
Crystal Seahorse, 51

D
Dana Point, 116
Dana Point Resort, 117
Dansk Tea Room, 200
Dar Maghreb Restaurant, 60
Deer Park, 206
Del Mar, 157
Di Stephanos, 60
Diaghilev, 47
Dining Room, The, 51
Dockside Cafe, 51
Dolphin Cruises, 35
Doryman's Inn, 94
Downey's, 32

E
Eagle's Landing, 133
Eagle's Nest, 135
Eiler's Inn, 107
El Bizcocho, 200
El Chalan Restaurant, 176
El Encanto, 25
Elario's Restaurant, 168

Ellen Scripps Browning Park, 174
Elsbree House, 181
Embarcadero Marina Park, 206
Encinitas, 151
Etienne's, 124

F

Falco, 207
Fanuel Street Park, 178
Fio's, 207
Firehouse Beach Cafe, 176
Fisherman's Restaurant and Bar,
    Oceanside, 149
Fisherman's Restaurant and Bar, San
    Clemente, 123
Five Crowns Restaurant, 104
Five Feet, 111
Fleur de Vin, 61
Fountainbleu Room, 196
Four Oaks Cafe, 61
Four Seasons Biltmore, Santa Barbara,
    26
Four Seasons Hotel, Newport Beach, 95
Franklin Murphy Sculpture Gardens,
    80
French Gourmet, 169

G

Gainey Vineyard, 20
Galaxy Park, 100
Garden House Inn, 128
Gaslamp Quarter, 207
Gaviota Beach, 22
Geoffrey's, 62
George's at the Cove, 169
George's Cafe and Bar, 170
George's Camelot, 96
Glenborough Inn, 27
Glenmore Plaza Hotel, 129
Glenn Park, 156

Glorietta Bay Inn, 185
Glorietta Bay Park, 178
Gold Mountain Manor, 134
Gondola East Getaways, 81
Grand Hotel, 19
Great American Balloon Company, 82
Griffith Park, 87
Gull House Bed and Breakfast, 129
Guy Fleming Trail, 175

H

Hamlet Garden Restaurant, 81
Harbor Beach, 149
Heap's Peak Arboretum, 137
Hearst Castle, 9
High Times, 82
Hill House, 192
Hilltop Stables, 189
Holly Street Bar and Grill, 83
Hollywood Roosevelt Hotel's Lobby
    Bar, The, 62
Horton Grand Hotel, 192
Horton Park Plaza Hotel, 195
Hotel Bel Air, 42
Hotel Del Coronado, 184
Hotel Laguna, 107
Hotel Shangri-La, 43
Huntington Library, 82

I

Ida Bailey's Restaurant, 193
Il Cielo, 63
Il Covo Coffeehouse, 170
Il Fornaio Restaurant, 160
Il Giardino, 64
Imperial Beach, 189
Ingleside Inn, 145
Ingrid's Cantina, 207
Inn at Fawnskin, 140
Inn at Laguna Beach, 108

Inn at Rancho Santa Fe, 158
Inn of Seventh Ray, 64
Inn on Mount Ada, 128
Insomniac, The, 207
Inspiration Point, 99
Invader Cruises, 179
Iron Squirrel, 140
Irvine Coast Charters, 100
Island Packers Company, 34

J
J'Adore, 65
J. Patrick House, 12
J. Paul Getty Museum, 83
Jake's Del Mar, 161
Java, 201
Julian, 212
Julian Farms Lodging, 215
Julian Grille, 218
Julian Hotel, 214
Julian White House, 215
Julienne, 83
JW's, 92

K
Kate Sessions Park, 178
King's Road Park, 100
Knickerbocker Mansion, 134

L
L'Auberge, 170
L'Auberge Del Mar, 157
L'Escale, 185
L'Escoffier, 68
L'Hirondelle, 121
L'Orangerie, 69
La Bonne Buffe, 152
La Chaumiere, 66
La Conversation, 66
La Grange, 67

La Jolla, 164
La Jolla Cove, 174
La Maida House and Bungalows, 44
La Marina, 26
La Sala Lounge, 26
La Tapenade, 194
La Valencia Hotel, 166
La Vie En Rose, 92
Laguna Beach, 105
Lake Arrowhead, 132
Lake San Marcos, 203
Lamont Street Grill, 177
Lantern Bay Park, 120
Las Brisas, 112
Le Bel Age, 47
Le Biarritz, 96
Le Chardonnay, 67
Le Meridian, 185
Le Petit Gourmet, 112
Le Valadon, 48
Little House on Bridge Street, 13
Living Room, The, 49
Loew's Santa Monica Beach Hotel, 45
Loma Vista Bed and Breakfast, 219
Los Angeles, 39
Los Olivos, 19
Louie's, 32
Lunaria, 70

M
Maison Magnolia, 70
Maison Robert's, 32
Malibu Beach Inn, 46
Malibu Country Inn, 46
Mansion Inn, 48
Marina Del Rey Hotel, 51
Marine Room, 171
Mattei's Tavern, 21
Mesa Lane Beach, 22
Miller's Acorn Ranch, 71

Milligan's, 171
Miracles, 154
Mission Bay, 179
Mission Bay Park, 180
Mission Beach, 179
Molly's, 201
Monica's, 71
Monique's Restaurant, 113
Montecito, 35
Moonstone Beach Drive,10
Mount Helix, 208
Mountain High Bed and Breakfast, 216
Mr. A's Restaurant, 202
Mr. Stox, 93

N
Newport Beach, 94
Nizetich's Restaurant, 72
Nucleus Nuance, 72

O
Ocean Beach, 181
Ocean Terrace, 170
Oceanfront Walk, 84
Oceanside, 149
Odyssey, 73
Old Turner Inn, 129
Old Yacht Club Inn, 27
Omelette Parlor, 74
One Rodeo, 55
Oyster's, 33

P
Pacific Beach, 176
Pacific Dining Car, 74
Pacifica Del Mar, 161
Pacifica Grill, 204
Palm Springs, 143
Palm Springs Aerial Tramway, 146
Pannikin, Del Mar, 162

Pannikin, Encinitas, 151
Pannikin, La Jolla, 172
Papa Louie's, 75
Papaguyo's, 209
Partner's Bistro, 114
Pasquel, 97
Patio, 26
Pavilion Queen, 103
Pelican Cove Inn, 150
Peninsula Hotel, 49
Peohe's Restaurant, 187
Piatti, 203
Pinecroft Manor, 214
Pines Park, 121
Pioneer Boulangerie, 75
Pismo Beach, 16
Point Dume Beach, 85
Portofino Beach Hotel, 95
Portofino Restaurant, 152
Powerhouse Park, 178
Prego, 202
Primavera, 188
Primi, 76

Q
Quail Botanical Gardens, 153
Quails Inn, 203
Quigg's, 181

R
Radisson Bel Air Summit, 50
Ragazzi, 76
Rainwater's, 203
Rancho Valencia, 194
Randon Oaks Ranch, 216
Reef, The, 77
Refugio State Beach, 22
Regent Beverly Wilshire, 51
Remington's, 20
Renaissance Cafe, 110

Renato, 95
Rex-II Ristorante, 77
Ritz Carlton Laguna Niguel, 118
Ritz Carlton Marina Del Rey, 50
Ritz, The, 97
Rive Gauche, 78
Robins, 13
Rock Haus, 158
Romano's Dodge House Restaurant,
    218
Romantique Lakeview Lodge, 135
Rothschild, 104

S
Saddle Back Inn, 136
Saddle Peak Lodge, 78
Salt Creek Beach Park, 120
San Clemente, 122
San Diego, 191
San Diego Coast, 149
San Diego Pier Cafe, 209
San Diego Zoo, 208
San Elijo State Beach, 156
San Luis Obispo, 15
San Ysidro Ranch, 35
Sand Castle Restaurant, 53
Sand Pebbles Inn, 11
Sanford Winery, 20
Santa Barbara, 21
Sante Ristorante, 172
Scalini, 162
Scripp's Inn, 165
Sea Grove Park, 163
Sea Venture Hotel and Restaurant, 16
Seaport Village, 209
Shadow Mountain Ranch, 217
Simpson House Inn, 28
Skorpios, 44
Sky Forest Bed and Breakfast Inn, 137

Sky Room, 166, 173
Skysurfer, 164
Solvang, 17
Sorrento Grille, 111
Sow's Ear, 14
Spalshes, 109
Splashes Bar, 109
St. James Club Hotel, 52
Stephano's, 197
Stonehouse Restaurant, 36
Storybook Inn, 137
Studio Milano, 113
Sunset Cliffs, 183
Surf and Sand Hotel, 108
Swami's Park and Lookout, 157
Sycamore Mineral Springs, 15

T
Taryn's at the Track, 163
Tea Cozy, 14
Temecula, 219
Terrace Restaurant, The, 114
Terrace, The, 108
Tete-a-Tete, 100
Thee Bungalow, 182
Thee White House, 93
Tidelands Park, 178
Tiffany Inn, 28
Top Hat, 207
Top O' the Cove Restaurant, 174
Top of the Hillcrest, 68
Topanga Canyon, 85
Torrey Pines State Reserve, 175
Towers Restaurant and Bar, 109
Trees, 104
Tryst, 79
Tutte Mare, 203
21 Oceanfront, 98
Two Bunch Palms, 144

U

U.S. Grant Hotel, 195
Upham, The, 29
Upstairs Cafe, 173
Upstart Crow, 209

V

Venice Beach House, 52
View Lounge, Marriott Hotel, 98
Villa Rosa, 30
Villa Royale, 144
Village Market Restaurant, 115
Vines, 14

W

Watercolors, 118

Wattles Park, 86
Westgate Hotel, 195
Whale Watch, 88
Whale Watching, 35, 87
Whale Watching on the Condor, 35
Will Rogers State Park, 88
Willow Creek Inn, 138
Windansea Beach, 175
Windy Point Inn, 139
Wine Cask Restaurant, 33
Wine Touring, 20

Z

Zaca Mesa, 20
Zanzibar Coffeehouse, 177